Adam Fouracre
with Dave Urwin

GLASSSPIDERPUBLISHING

Cover design by Judith S. Design & Creativity
www.judithsdesign.com
Published by Glass Spider Publishing
www.glassspiderpublishing.com

This book is dedicated in loving memory of Lloyd Fouracre (1987-2005).
Also, to Ben, for all you've had to put up with over the years!

Introduction

"What do you want?!"

Of course, I would have chosen my words more carefully had I known what I was about to hear. It was shortly after midnight on 25th September 2005, and I was due to work a long shift on my nurse training in the morning. The phone was on the other side of the room, and so I had to leave the warmth of my bed to go and shut the noise off. What's more, I couldn't make out a word my dad was saying. The connection was bad, and seeing as I had barely woken up, it felt like this was his fault. It didn't occur to me at the time that if he was ringing me in the middle of the night, it must be with good reason. I was annoyed.

The signal finally cleared, and for the first time, I realised he was crying. Oh, no, what could it be? Mum? Nan?

"It's Lloyd. He's been attacked," he sobbed, and took a while to get the words out: "He's dead."

There it was. The moment that changed the course of my life. Those two words are the reason I'm writing this book. The reason I've dedicated so much of myself to a single cause. At first, it didn't sink in. How could it? I went to bed knowing that I had a brother but hadn't even thought about it. Why would I? It was just a fact about me; there was no reason to reaffirm it to myself before going to bed. Now I was hearing my dad cry for the first time, and my tired brain was trying to process the fact that I was living in a world without Lloyd—the brother I had grown up with.

Going back to sleep was obviously out of the question, and Dad had told me that the police were on the way to take me to meet them at the hospital, so I got dressed in a hurry and made my way downstairs. My housemate was still up.

"Hey, Adam, what are you doing up?" he said as he turned away from whatever he was watching on TV and looked me in the eye. "I thought you had work in the morning."

"I did," I replied blankly, "but I just found out my brother's been murdered."

He had nothing to say to that, but I had nothing to add, and it was a relief when he left the room after an awkward silence. I just stood and waited for the police officer to arrive as I paced back and forth. My footsteps seemed loud in the stillness of night. How was I supposed to act? I should have been wailing on the floor or throwing things around the room. If this were a film, that's just what my character would be doing, but I just felt numb.

Before long, my parents arrived, my dad explaining that they had been asked to leave by the police because Lloyd was now part of a crime scene, and instead we would be going to my grandparents' house. I was still just going with the flow and agreed that this was what we would do. Later on, I did regret the fact that I hadn't been able to see Lloyd that night and to say goodbye then. He would have been in a horrific state. He was brutally beaten up by some drunken youths and died from his injuries, but at least he would still have been warm.

My nan made us all a cup of tea when we arrived. What else could she do? We were all just in shock. I remember when my nan and me were alone together at one point, perhaps I was helping her carry the tea through and she told me that I shouldn't let my parents see me cry. These words have stuck with me ever since. Unfortunately, I have always found it difficult since then to show emotion. Every time I feel upset or start to well up, I hear a little voice in my head saying, "Don't be so weak! You look like a fool!" or something like that, and I'll stop straight away. I rarely cry nowadays, and I guess I could come across as being quite a cold person, but it's only because I got so used to hiding the tears from my parents. There have been a few times I couldn't hold it back, but by and large, I put up a barrier around that time that has still not come down.

In the early days after Lloyd's death, my mum would cry all the time, and I couldn't help feeling embarrassed when she did it in public. Not because I thought she was weak. In fact, when I think of it now, I was nineteen and should have known better. I just hated people staring because they wouldn't know why some random woman had started crying. I had no confidence, and I had always hated being the centre of attention, so as selfish as it was, I wished she would stop and we could leave. I just didn't know how to make things better. My dad became quite withdrawn and shut himself away quite a bit. We lived in the middle of nowhere and I didn't drive, so I floated around the house and made myself scarce when there was a lot of crying going on, my nan's words coming back to me every time. People would visit the house with cards and flowers, and I would always be the one to answer the door even though I was never the person people were coming to see. I remember opening the door to several people who would express their apologies and ask me if I was okay, but no sooner could I form the answer than they had disappeared into the front room to comfort my crying mum. I felt like a family butler with no real purpose and was just drifting, not having any idea what I was meant to do next.

Nobody teaches you in school what you should do when a family member is suddenly taken from you in the most shocking and brutal way. Most people are lucky never to have to experience it. In one single moment, I went from being a young lad beginning his life with minimal worries to a broken young man with the weight of the world on his shoulders. Nothing prepares you for that.

Jay: One

Did I mean to kill someone that night?

No. I can say with my hand on my heart that it was never my intention. But did I mean to hurt someone? Unfortunately, yes, I did. Because I acted upon my intention, life will never be the same again for me, or for the family of the lad who got hurt because of me.

Nothing was unusual about that day, to begin with. I was a young man, and I did what many young men do at the weekend. I played football in the day, and later on I would go out drinking to celebrate a friend's sister's birthday.

I was feeling great when I first went out because the football match couldn't have gone much better. I hadn't started the game because I'd been suspended a while back when my temper got me sent off in a previous game, but I came on as a substitute and scored the winning goal.

It seems strange to think now that earlier that day I'd been the hero. I was buzzing from that, I guess, and I remember walking with a few friends from Priorswood, the area of Taunton I lived in at the time, to the Staplegrove Inn.

It was a 25-minute walk, give or take. We had a couple of spliffs before we went to the pub, and there was nothing tense about the atmosphere, to begin with. We were just having a good time.

The drinks were flowing, as they always were back then on the weekend. I wouldn't call myself an alcoholic, but when I drank it was always to get drunk; I would never just have a few.

The atmosphere changed as the evening went on. A couple more friends came along later and there was already tension between them. I don't really know what the issue was, but words were exchanged, and you could tell they weren't friendly ones. I'd been chatting with this girl who'd just split up with her boyfriend, and things became awkward when he turned up. Her dad was there, and he smoothed things over, but a few of the lads gave me some stick over it. At first, I could laugh it off, but when lads hang out together they sometimes don't know when to let things go, especially when there's drink involved. I felt like they were mugging me off, and it was all a bit unnecessary. I was trying to get this girl's number, and there was no need for them to get in the way of that. I wasn't feeling angry, though, just a little bit irritated with some of the lads, and it didn't ruin my night. I was still having a good time up until that point.

Not long after this, a window got smashed by one of the guys we were with. It was all innocent; he was just banging on the window to get someone's attention but, probably because he was drunk, he banged harder than he meant to, and the glass smashed. The guy behind the bar wanted him to apologise, and to pay for the damage, and again there were words exchanged. Nobody was shouting, but we obviously weren't welcome anymore and so we decided to leave before somebody tried to make us.

The mood had definitely shifted from when we'd arrived at the pub. There were five of us still left when we walked away down Greenway Road, which leads back towards Priorswood: myself and my friends Lee, John, Andrew, and Gary. There had been a few small arguments throughout the day and so there was simmering tension. We were all friends, but we were 19, we'd been drinking for hours and we all had anger lying dormant in us for different reasons. Any one of us could have erupted at any time if someone had said or done the wrong thing. I bumped into my friend John by accident and within an instant, we were scrapping on the floor. I don't know how or why it happened, but things escalated so quickly. I don't know about him, but I had no interest in winning the fight; I just knew it shouldn't be happening. Normally we got on so well. I could walk into his house at any time, or he could walk into mine, and we got on well with each other's mums. We were almost like family. He managed to get the upper hand and I was pinned underneath him, but I had no thoughts of hurting him, only that I wanted the fight to be over. I managed to push him off and then called an end to it.

He didn't pursue it any further and I was glad, but my pride was hurt. He'd had the better of the scuffle and that touched a nerve in me. I made a snap decision there and then that I was gonna get in a fight with someone else. I was angry, but I didn't want to take it out on my friend, even though it was because of a fight with him that I felt the way I did. Someone else was gonna get hurt. I didn't care who it was, but I was gonna hit someone. I just wanted to hurt them. That's all. I just wanted to punch someone to the ground and restore my pride. I wanted to get the better of someone physically because John had got the better of me. I never thought for a second of ending anyone's life or even seriously injuring them.

Before I knew it, I was on my own near Staplegrove Hockey Club, which was new at the time, and I saw a couple of guys walking towards me. My friends had kept walking, but I barely even noticed. I just knew in my head I was about to fight. I don't remember the exact sequence of events from that moment. I'm not sure if it's because of the alcohol or because of what my decision would come to mean, but there are definite gaps in my memory. I remember throwing a couple of punches at this guy, I don't remember if he hit me back, but I called my friends back and made sure everyone else was involved. I've gone over and over it all in my head since and all I think I can remember is a sound. I now know that sound was my friend hitting another lad with a wooden sign.

I didn't know what I was doing. It's no excuse, but I made a mistake. It's that simple. Everyone makes mistakes, but mine caused more pain to more people than I could ever have imagined. I only wanted someone to feel a little bit of pain and humiliation like I had. Everything happened very quickly and there was a lot going on. I remember someone rolling on the floor and I kicked him and was shouting at him, then someone else was on the floor nearby, who I now know was a lad named Lloyd Fouracre. I stamped on him and I think I punched him while he was on the ground. There was a lot of shouting, then suddenly some car headlights came very close and so we ran. I don't remember seeing any blood at the time, but maybe if I'd seen what happened to Lloyd, I would have registered the seriousness of the situation.

We ran off in different directions, but John and Andrew ran the same way as me. I felt no sense of panic, or of having been responsible for something that would change my whole life. The way I saw it we'd just given some lads a bit of a kicking and we were running so we didn't have to face the consequences. They might be a bit sore the next day, but it would soon be forgotten about if we kept our heads down for a bit. We didn't know the people we'd fought with, and there was nothing linking them to us. We just had a bit of a drunken ruck. It happens.

I could not have been more wrong, and instead of everything going back to normal the next day life would change forever, for me and for many people, just because I started a fight. You might think a fight is no big deal. I'm telling this story so you know how wrong you might be.

Let's Start

I didn't get to see Lloyd on the night he died; my parents made it to the hospital in time to be with him when he breathed his last, but then they were asked to leave by the police. They would have given me the choice if they had been able to. My brother was considered to be "evidence" and so he had to be taken away until the forensics team had done what they needed to. I'm not sure what difference it would have made, and you may wonder why I would even have wanted to see him lying battered in a hospital bed. The thought only really began to play on my mind after I was allowed to see him a while later. His body had been taken and an autopsy had been carried out along with other forensic examinations. What remained was just a shell of the brother I'd known. I could never adequately explain what it felt like to watch him lying lifeless in the coffin. It is something that could only ever be known through experience, although I would not wish it upon anyone.

We were all in two minds about going to see Lloyd at the hospital once more, but the thought of missing the opportunity and then being filled with regret meant we couldn't say no. I knew I had to be there, but I was completely unprepared for the massive dose of reality I was about to be faced with. Just entering the room was enough to shatter my composure. The brother I'd grown up with was there, but the instant I saw him it struck me how he was no longer a part of this world and never would be again. My reaction shocked me as much as the sight of Lloyd did; a flood of tears erupted as I shook and gasped for breath. It was like a passing heavy rain-storm; short-lived but hideously violent. I quickly got back in control of my emotions and took another glance at Lloyd. He was a mess. His jaw was broken, and it made his face seem deformed. His eyes were shut tight, his skin ghostly pale and his posture rigid. I wanted to remember him as his hair-gelled, lively, cheeky self but the last image I would ever have of him was of this lifeless husk.

This was my reality now. I couldn't stay in this room indefinitely, neither did I much want to, even though I had no idea what to do next. I had a few images in my head of characters in films who said goodbye to loved ones with a kiss on the forehead. I decided pretty quickly that this was what I would do, but instead of being the fitting farewell I intended, it became a horrific memory I will probably never shake off. I leant forward and kissed Lloyd on the forehead, but as soon as my lips touched his marble-like skin I felt my core temperature plummeting. He felt so cold that I could only liken it to the "life force'" being drained from me. I recoiled in shock and was filled with sadness and confusion. How could my own brother make me feel so chilled to the core?

This shouldn't be happening. He was only 17, but this wasn't even Lloyd anymore. He never even got to turn 18. This shell of a young man that remained would not have any more birthdays, would never see the sun rise or set, would never have another conversation with me or anyone else . . . it was just too much to take in. This was it. No more Lloyd. He'd had a lot of friends, and a promising career ahead of him. I'm sure he would have made our parents very proud, and I'm sure we would have always remained close, but we will never know. Everything Lloyd was and everything he ever would be left this world in 2005.

I thought back to when we were younger, and how I'd always tried to protect him despite the brotherly quarrels we had. My mother, Helen, and my father, Simon, were driven to distraction at times by our constant bickering. It's probably the same for most parents of young boys, but our neighbours would quite often be shocked by the sight of me trapping Lloyd's head in the clothes horse in the back garden or painting him with yellow gloss. I was a little older than him and so I often had the better of our arguments, but he would usually get his own back in the end. My mum was usually the one who got exasperated with us, my dad was a lot more laid back. They made a well-rounded match, and together they decided that we would learn by taking responsibility for our own actions. I quickly learnt where the boundaries were when I threw an egg at a passing car one day and the police turned up on our doorstep shortly afterwards! This was the last time I had anything to do with the police until after Lloyd died.

Despite our arguments, we were always close, and when I think back to our early childhood it just seems so unfair the way things turned out. Is it ever fair to lose a family member way before their time though? We had a pretty idyllic childhood compared to many, growing up in a tiny place called Cushuish Lane, just outside the village of Kingston St Mary. It was nestled in the outskirts of the Quantock Hills outside Taunton, the "big city" where Lloyd's life would be cruelly taken from him. Taunton is the biggest town in that area of Somerset, but Cushuish is a single lane with just a few houses in the middle of nowhere. There was a huge Oak tree in the hedgerow directly opposite our house. It had colossal roots winding around the hedge, which was almost hollow inside, and so was perfect for firing the imaginations of two tiny children. It was almost like we were on our way to Narnia!

We did have skateboards, so we were pretty cool, but not cool enough to try and stand up on them! We knelt on them instead, as if we were on surfboards and waiting to catch waves, but actually we were just too scared to stand. Some older kids who lived down the lane did introduce us to a nearby dip in the road where we could pick up some speed. Most of the other kids nearby were older, but we did have some friends and never felt isolated despite being out in the sticks.

When I was 7 years old, we left the tranquillity of Cushuish for the bright lights of Broomfield . . . Broomfield is an even smaller, sparser village, and we were still on the outskirts now with only three other houses nearby! It is definitely not a bustling metropolis, although it is home to the well-known Fyne Court National Trust property. Lloyd was quite a sickly child, even spending a few nights in A&E after asthma attacks. One night when he was about 8 or 9, he woke up and instantly vomited all over himself and his bed sheets and started crying. I managed to settle him down and get him cleaned up. Our parents slept through the whole episode. I guess I knew then I was likely going to train as a nurse.

Nothing about our life in Broomfield suggested what was to come. My favourite memory from then was when we found a cat in the holly bush at the top of the field near our house, not long after we moved in. I've never been much of a cat lover but this one I thought was awesome straight away. We kept finding it in the same place time and time again, and after a while we encouraged it down to the house with some food. Eventually, it came in and we became its adopted family. We wanted to call it Holly, due to where it was found, but the vet told us he was a boy and so he became Olly. He used to walk with us to the school bus and would then be waiting in the same place for us when we came back hours later. I don't know if he stayed in the same place all day, but he was always there, and he quickly became our best friend.

I had an unwritten rule that nobody but me was allowed to beat Lloyd up, and this was put to the test on one of our family holidays. We would go away out of season or on Sun voucher holidays because we never had much money . . . or because my parents were cheapskates, but I loved our excursions to River Dart Country Park. There was a tunnel slide that you had to go down on a sack, so Lloyd and I set up all the bags at the bottom of the slide so we could burst through them. Lloyd was on his way to the top of the slide to take his turn when a kid who gave off a strange vibe came over and tried to set fire to the sacks.

"What are you doing?" I gasped.

"Be quiet; it's funny," he said. I was stunned for a second but then I saw that the bags were alight, and I knew Lloyd would be coming down the slide at any moment, so I ran over and frantically stamped them out.

"What are you doing?" growled the kid, not seeming to understand that I was trying to protect my brother from being seriously hurt, only thinking that I had ruined his fun. The next thing I knew, Lloyd was at the bottom of the slide and the kid started shoving him around. I've never been a tough guy, in fact I'm usually the total opposite, but the red mist descended, and I picked up handfuls of gravel, throwing them at the other kid as hard as I could.

"Get away from my brother!" I yelled as I pelted him with handful after handful of gravel. He ran away, and he got a further pelting from my dad when we spotted him later on, but only a verbal one this time.

Years later, nobody was able to frighten off Lloyd's attackers with fistfuls of gravel; sadly, it was way beyond that. One of Lloyd's friends bravely attempted to wrestle one of his attackers to the ground but got a kicking for his trouble. There was not much any of his friends could have done; they were in the wrong place at the wrong time and came across a volatile group who were intent on causing somebody harm.

I felt like I was falling apart, but my grandmother's words from the other night came back to me and my tears stopped before they could even reappear. I stopped to consider how my parents must be feeling. My mum had carried Lloyd for 9 months, then she and my dad had raised him together. They'd watched him grow from a baby to a young man, and he had so much ahead of him, but it was all taken away in an instant because of a mindless attack. I tried to put myself in their shoes and I just couldn't begin to imagine what losing a son must feel like. He was my brother and I loved him. I really did; he was like the other half of me, but I didn't raise him. I didn't sacrifice so much to make sure he had the opportunities I wished I did. The trauma was unimaginable, and my parents had looked after me, after us, so much over the years. Now it was my turn to try and look after them.

The gravity of the responsibility that was now on my shoulders hit me for the first time. My parents would get older, and if nothing happened to me in the meantime, I would lose them one day. Lloyd would not be there to share my grief. For just a moment I thought to share a joke with him.

"You won't even be there to help me choose their care home," I smiled, but this was just a momentary glimmer amid the darkness. The future just seemed scary without Lloyd being a part of it. I saw little of the hope, excitement, and opportunities I had been imagining just a few weeks previously. Frankly, I was terrified.

Jay: Two

For some reason, when we were running off we cut through some allotments off to the side of the path. We could have kept going down the path we were on, and it probably would have been quicker, but we had taken a diversion. I'd lost my shoe in a ditch somewhere, and before long I had kicked off the other one. I wasn't thinking about getting rid of evidence. It was just because I'd lost one and it was easier to run barefoot than with one shoe on. I could have easily found the other shoe and picked it up, but for some reason, I didn't. All the lads who I'd been with had scattered in different directions, but I was with John and Andrew. I don't know why we had run off together.

I was beginning to sober up quite quickly by this point. We'd been in a fight, and although at the time I had no idea how badly anyone had been hurt it was enough to bring me pretty sharply back to reality. I was beginning to become a bit more aware of my surroundings,

I was walking up the road barefoot with John, Andrew had gone another way, but we were all going to meet up back at Lee's. His parents weren't there that night, and neither were his kid brother and sister, so that was where we'd arranged to meet. I'm not sure what time it was when we got there but it wasn't far from the allotment and so it didn't take long. Lee was there with his older sister and her friend, and we all sat down, still not being aware of how much trouble we might be in. I must have been quite a strange sight. I was barefoot, and I had a load of cider and black down my top. Maybe there was blood there too. I'm not sure. There probably was some blood on my jeans but they were dark, so you couldn't really see it. I just remember looking down and seeing pink on my t-shirt.

We smoked some weed and chatted a bit about what had gone on, but we just said we'd been in a fight and we probably talked about the window being smashed in the pub too. The atmosphere was really quite chilled, but then after a while, Gary turned up.

"That was serious," he said. "I think that kid was pretty badly hurt."

I kind of brushed it off. Looking back now I may just have been in denial, but I really don't think I believed anyone had been seriously harmed. Not long after Gary walked in, Andrew arrived. There was a music channel on the TV and there was an image of a coffin in one of the videos.

"That's what that kid's gonna be in!" said Andrew. At the time I thought nothing much of it because that was just the culture of the group I hung out with. They thought it was pretty cool to have been in a fight, and everyone would always say things like that to try and sound tough. They thought there was a certain amount of respect that went along with being a bit "tasty," so I just took it as a bit of bravado. Looking back now, though, it seems like such a messed-up thing to say, and I wonder if he knew what he'd done.

When I think back to that night years later, I feel so far removed from who I was then, and the kind of life I was living just seems so pointless. Of course I'm quite a bit older now and most people change their outlook on life as the years go by and you experience more in life, but I can see that I had no real direction and was a ticking time bomb. The people I was spending time with were only really interested in drinking and fighting, and so that's where I was in life as well.

I didn't get back home until around six in the morning. I'd borrowed some trainers and walked home, which wasn't far. I don't remember thinking much about what had happened on the way back, just about how nice it would be to go to bed. It was really early, but I knocked on the door because I didn't have a key with me, and my mum's partner answered. I could see the concern on his face straight away, but maybe I didn't really take it in because I was tired and just wanted to sleep.

"Jay, what have you done?" he said. "The police are looking for you."

Again, I just shrugged it off. I was still feeling pretty stoned despite the walk back, and I was pretty deluded about life at that point anyway, so I didn't take what he'd said seriously. I went to bed and dozed off almost straight away.

When I woke up a bit later my foot was in agony. I could barely move, but I managed to get to the bathroom and ran some hot water. Now it was the morning after, and I'd sobered up completely, I began to replay the events of the night before in my head. What if someone had been really hurt? What if he was in hospital? I could actually be in a bit of trouble. To be completely honest I didn't feel bad that I might have hurt someone, just worried that I might be in bother.

When I'd got dressed my mum's husband tried to talk to me again.

"Come on, Jay," he said. "I've got to take you to the police station."

"Nah, that's not happening!" I replied and went out on my bike. My foot was still in a bad way and I couldn't play football, so I just went back to Lee's. I stepped into the back garden and heard a deep voice that I didn't recognise. When I looked through the window, I saw a police officer, and I instinctively ducked out of view. I didn't have a plan of how I would stay away from them forever; it was just a standard flight response. I slipped out before anyone could see me and got on my bike, quickly heading off towards the park to watch the football. On the way there I passed the other end of the lane where the fight had happened. It was cordoned off with police tape and there was a patrol car parked nearby. I began to go through the possibilities in my head of what might have happened, but it never once crossed my mind that someone might have lost their life. Deep down I knew I'd caused something serious through my actions, but I didn't want to face up to it.

At the football match I talked to a few friends about what had happened, but I just told the story as if it was a normal fight. I didn't tell anyone that I was worried someone might be in a critical condition. After a while, I got a text from my mum's partner saying that the police had turned up at home and I had to go back. I replied, saying, "Okay, I'm on my way back."

I don't know if I would have gone back so quickly if I'd known what I would be met with, but I knew that whatever it was I'd have to face up to it sooner or later.

I was in Staplegrove, which isn't far from where I was living in Priorswood, so I got back there in no time and the police were waiting. It was pretty naïve of me to think they would tell me anything other than what they were going to, but I was a kid of nineteen and at that age, you don't realise how serious the consequences of your actions might be.

"Jay Wall, I'm arresting you for murder," the police officer stated.

With those words, my heart just sank. I didn't panic, I didn't think to run, I didn't cry. I had none of the responses you might have thought I would. It just hit me for the first time that this was serious, and it would change my life. The reality of what I hadn't wanted to accept came to the surface. Those words are just too much to take in when you don't even realise what you've done. I didn't know anyone had died, and I don't think it even sank in straight away. All I knew was that I was in a lot of trouble.

It was the last time I remember being out in the community until after my 30th birthday had come and gone.

Playing the Part

"What's your reason for not coming in?" barked the nurse who took my call. I'd been trying to persevere with my nursing studies but that day I just couldn't face it. Nursing is a stressful profession, and if any staff member is absent it does put something of a strain on the others. This was no ordinary situation, though; my brother had recently been murdered. I expected a little understanding at the very least, especially as I'd gone to the effort of pretending to cry in anticipation of her frosty response.

"I'm sorry," I began. "I've had a really difficult time lately. You see . . ."

"I'm aware of your situation, Adam," she said, her voice devoid of emotion, which stopped me in my tracks. "When will you be back?"

I couldn't quite believe what I was hearing. You think of nursing as such a caring profession, but I was treated like I was a nuisance. It had been the same on the days I had been in. Nobody had treated me any differently, even though they were all aware of what had happened. Admittedly it must have been hard to know how to respond to me. Maybe they thought I'd find it easier if they tried to be normal around me than if they were constantly fussing over me.

They were correct, but they were being a little too normal, and it showed. There was no allowance, concession, or display of understanding, nobody checking that I was okay. Situations change hour to hour in nursing, people get better or become more unwell, especially as I was on the acute medical unit looking after very poorly people. It was emotionally challenging and very fast-paced. I didn't expect fussing but what I did expect was that if I needed time out then this was understood, no questions asked.

There were a number of times when I felt like collapsing on the ward floor. I was so tired and was completely lacking in motivation. In recent years it's been easy to look back and see that I was depressed, but at the time nobody picked up on this, myself included, because I wouldn't talk about how I was feeling, and to be honest nobody really cared or took the time to find out. My mum was always able to express how she was feeling, she was regularly sent for breaks or sent home if she was struggling because she cried or the grief was clear to see. I didn't cry and I guess that's why everyone thought I was okay. It seemed that in order to be treated with compassion you had to "play the part" of the grieving brother of a murder victim and it sucked. This was the reason I used to try and fake cry, just so I wouldn't be made to feel awful, more awful than I already did. With hindsight, I can comfortably say that the expectations from other people were one of the hardest things to balance and cope with than the grief itself.

It wasn't just the hospital; it was college, too. I remember we were supposed to be prepping a presentation to give to the group. This had been set after my brother had died and when I was supporting my family and being briefed daily by the police. I'm not sure whether the court case had happened or not at this stage. I had put together the parts of the presentation that I was due to complete, but I had missed a few of the practice sessions with the group I was working with. Until this point, I had got on well with all in my friendship group, but something had changed over this time. I used to lift share with one of the ladies in the group and over time the journeys became tense, something not spoken, clearly there was a gripe she had with me but was not prepared to voice it just to irritate me with her disdain. I tried asking the others in the group, but I was nervous and didn't want to ask directly. Suddenly, one of the girls in the group exploded.

"We are all pissed off, Adam, because you haven't been pulling your weight for this presentation!"

"We know your brother has died but we all have challenges with home life, I have kids to juggle childcare for, and we all make it to practices! You need to get over it!"

I was stunned, I didn't know what to say. They stormed off and left me in front of a courtyard full of other students. I melted and found a staircase to curl up on. I was so angry and embarrassed that I wept. One of the other girls from my class had witnessed it all and came over to me and asked if I was okay. She really helped to give me some security in that moment. Clearly, she also informed the course leaders as I was swiftly taken into a room and asked about my disgraceful encounter with the group now termed "The Three Witches."

I have always wondered how they could have been so cruel, why they didn't talk through any issues before that point. I saw one of them a few years later. She was walking into one of the supermarkets I was collecting outside of. I caught her eye and she put her nose in the air and pretended to ignore me. I have no idea why I did it, but I went over and said, "I'm sorry we fell out and for causing upset." She stopped and instantly changed.

"It's okay", she said. "We were all just so worried about you and we just wanted you to talk to us, but you wouldn't. It was so frustrating for us." I wasn't quite sure what to say to this. Frustrating for you? Once again it came down to expectations. They expected some major drama from me that they could support me in. They wanted an *Eastenders*-esque storyline to be playing out in college—lovely! Were they wanting to support me? Or were they wanting something for themselves, something to make them feel part of the drama or be needed? I have no idea; all I do know is people can be weird.

On the day of Lloyd's funeral, I was able to banish some of the horror of the previous time I'd seen him because this time he was in his own clothes and had they'd gelled his hair. He looked more like himself for sure. His coffin had already been loaded into the hearse when we arrived, and we were able to see him one final time. He had a little more colour than he had before and was a bit more like the Lloyd I wanted to remember. I wished he would open his eyes and be the cheeky git he could be at times. He sometimes used to call me a faggot in jest. I had come out as gay when I was 16, and Lloyd was the first person I told, but he happened to have a friend with him at the time as well. We were on holiday and I'd been drinking, so I just blurted it out. I had expected a grimace or some comment from Lloyd for the benefit of his friend, but he just said "So what? You are still, and always will be, my brother." Maybe he'd already guessed. He would make cheeky comments later on, but it was only ever brotherly banter.

My dad actually twigged without me even having to tell him. He locked me in the car one day after he'd picked me up from school (just locked the doors with me in the passenger seat; he didn't bundle me into the boot!) and told me that I wasn't getting out until I told him what was wrong. I wasn't having any of it. I gave him the silent treatment and tried to make my escape, but as I wrestled with the door lock, he said "Do you want me to tell you what I think the matter is?" He knew. I told him that he was right, and he said it was probably just a phase but if I knew I was gay then I was still his son and his opinion of me would never change. He even sent me a card a little while later reaffirming what he'd said. I was so touched to receive it.

I was still hoping to have a "normal" family some day and so I wanted my dad to be right about it only being a phase, but I became more certain over time and so I wrote everything in a letter to my parents and put it in an envelope. I then left it in their room so they could read it in their own time. I tried to go to bed afterwards, but of course I was only thinking of them opening the letter and imagining all of the possible outcomes. Sleep was never going to happen, and after a while they both came in and sat on the end of my bed, explaining that this changed nothing for them and that they loved me just the same. Most experiences I've had when it comes out that I'm gay have been positive, but one potential sponsor for the charity I later founded went bright red and excused himself when I let slip that my partner was a man, and I never heard from him again. Towards the end of school, I had a crush on another pupil who didn't take kindly to the news and said that he wanted to kill me. Hopefully, he didn't mean it. My current partner Ben, who I have now married, I had not actually known for long when Lloyd died, and he stuck around despite everything, so I knew he was genuine from the start.

My school years were definitely not a positive experience for me. It all began at primary school in Kingston St. Mary, where the head teacher was a bit of a bully. He never abused me physically, but he undermined me in a number of ways over the years. I never knew what I'd done wrong, and so I was desperate to impress him, but the more I tried the more he belittled me, which ground down my confidence over time. I was always quite a sensitive child, but he often called me a "chimp" in front of my classmates, and Lloyd would encourage the other pupils to call me names, which was how he got his own back after I'd got the better of our arguments at home. I thought my chance had come to win the head teacher's respect when I was finally chosen to tidy the PE cupboard, a task that pupils took it in turns to be assigned to. I always volunteered but was never chosen, until finally, it was my turn. Usually, we would be put in pairs to complete the task, but I would be on my own. I was pleased because then he would know it was all my effort, and I was determined to do a great job so he couldn't possibly find fault with me.

I gave the task my all and came back to classroom knowing that I couldn't have done any better. I was delighted to see when I walked in that a picture I'd drawn had been pinned up on the wall. It seemed that I was finally getting some recognition for my efforts, but sadly I would soon find out from one of my classmates that when I'd been tidying the PE cupboard, the teacher had been explaining to the class how my work was terrible and was an example of how not to do the task. It was as if he had got me out of the way so he could give the others more ammunition to tease me. It was done in such a subtle and underhand way, which made it all the more painful. Compared to some of the things I would go through later in life this was nothing, but for a 10-year-old boy who was already starting to doubt himself, it was a crushing blow.

Things didn't get much easier as I moved up to Secondary School. I was pretty terrified of the thought of moving to the tough old town when I'd been at a quiet school in a small village and even that had not been easy. What's more, I had begun to put on weight as soon as I hit puberty. I had never worried about body image previously, but one day I took my shirt off on the football field only to be met with jibes and laughter, so I put it straight back on. From then on, I would try to avoid any kind of similar situations. I even went off swimming, when before it had been one of my favourite activities. PE was always a nightmare from then on, and my new school was something of a culture shock. I heard language I had not heard before and was interacting with children who seemed tougher and more streetwise.

I was not really bullied in Secondary School. Of course there was teasing, but I didn't get it any worse than anyone else really. I have to say also that the girls were worse than the boys. Lloyd and I still had our fights and rows during those years, but by the time I moved out of home when I was 16, he had grown into the kind of young man anyone would want as a brother. Joining the Air Cadets was a big part of this I think, and he was very dedicated; they were absolutely full of praise for him. He was very cheeky, but after I'd moved out our friendship went from strength to strength. We hadn't always been at each other's throats growing up, but we had more of a love/hate relationship. When we met up in 2005, we would get on superbly, and instead of winding each other up, we would complain about our parents, as teenagers tend to. We would often still have Sunday lunch at the family home, and Lloyd would kindly offer to pick me up in his car. I was unable to drive because of my epilepsy.

My condition was long-standing, but I first experienced a fit at the age of 15, and the whole experience probably brought Lloyd and me closer. Nothing seemed unusual about the day, and I'd just been playing a computer game when I suddenly felt my muscles twitching and my head spinning. I had previously been made aware of the signs by the doctor, and I knew what was happening, but I felt powerless to stop it. The next thing I remember is being walked down the stairs by a frantic Lloyd. He was terrified that I was going to die from a brain haemorrhage, as one of his friends had the year before. He had found me collapsed on my bedroom floor. I could taste blood in my mouth, and I worked out sometime later that I had bitten my tongue. I barely remember another thing from that day, except that my parents had been out, and Lloyd had called them, so they rushed straight back. I remember them getting in, but nothing that was said, or whether I was taken to hospital.

Epilepsy was still quite a big problem until I was 24. It never stopped me from living my life day to day, but it's only been in recent years I've been allowed to drive again, and I've never been put on the early morning shift at work because it was established over time that this seemed to be a trigger. I have a full driving license nowadays, but until quite recently I had to have it reviewed every three years. I experienced a number of tonic-clonic seizures when I was younger but have not had one in years, and I think I have the condition under control. I am grateful to Lloyd for looking after me that first day I had a fit. He was so upset and was genuinely concerned that he was going to lose me.

The first time Lloyd picked me up for Sunday lunch I found out that he had an ulterior motive. He'd recently started a part-time cleaning job in some local offices, and he roped me in to help him on our way over to our parents' house. I was tasked with emptying the bins! I didn't really mind, though, because we were able to have conversations we wouldn't be able to have during lunch, and we got on well, so despite the unexpected work shift, it was just a chance to hang out with my brother. I appreciate that day even more in light of what was soon to follow.

I dropped out of college after my first year and was quite directionless in life at the time, but when I was 18, I decided to work as a health care assistant as I felt that a career in health care might be for me. Turns out it was, so I signed up to undertake my Diploma in adult nursing. I'm sure Lloyd would have had a great career too, judging by his dedication to the Air Cadets. We will never know, but it could just as easily have been me who was brutally attacked. In fact, I was involved in a very similar incident just a few months previously. I had been walking home from a friend's house late at night and was crossing over Hamilton Road in Taunton when I spotted a group of lads who looked like the ones news reports at the time told you to keep away from. They were just loitering by the side of the road and my instinct told me to go another way, but then I changed my mind. I thought I was being prejudiced, and that they weren't interested in me, so I carried on the same way.

As I walked past, they jeered, but I had my headphones on and so I just kept walking. Suddenly, though, one of the group was right in my face and squaring up to me. I turned and began to walk quickly in the other direction. As I did, I thought I saw a knife in one of their hands, so I was terrified. I couldn't really run because I had a heavy backpack. I had barely gone a few steps when I felt a thumping blow to the back of my head, and I fell forward. I tried to get back to my feet but then punches rained down on me from several members of the group. Fortunately, I was carrying a thick coat, so I was able to put it over my head whilst they kicked and stamped on me, just as the group who attacked Lloyd had done to him. I was able to protect my head, but all the same, I was dazed. My vision had become a blur, and my legs were like jelly. Luckily, they got bored pretty quickly and thought they had made their point. I got out of the way of an approaching car and tried to rush home as quickly as I could. A passer-by, one of several who were just stood on the pavement staring, asked me if I was okay as I was leaving the area, but I didn't stop because I thought it was a bit late for anyone to intervene, and I just wanted to get back.

My housemate was still up when I got in and I told him what had happened. He made me report it to the police straight away, even though I wasn't too keen, and an officer came to take my statement. He asked me if I would be able to identify my attacker if we drove out to where it had happened, and I said I would.

"You'll just drive past so I can point him out, though, right?" I said. "We won't have to get out and talk to them?"

"Oh, no," he assured me. "Of course not."

The group of lads were in pretty much exactly the same place they had been before. They had not seemed concerned about getting in trouble for what they had done to me, and none of them had run off when they got bored of hitting me at the time. It seemed that nobody had reported the incident in the meantime, because they were acting as if nothing had happened.

"That's them," I said, and the police officer nodded. I thought he would drop me back again before coming back with a couple of colleagues to talk to the group, but he pulled up right next to them! I looked at him in disbelief, but he was already halfway out of the car.

"Is this the one?" he said, nodding in the direction of the ringleader of the group. I couldn't believe what was happening, but at least the lads weren't stupid enough to attack me again in front of a police officer.

A few days later an identity line-up was arranged, but I arrived only to be told that the line-up had been the day before. I knew there was a mistake because I had written down the date and time of the line-up as soon as I had been given it, knowing that I would forget otherwise. I tried to explain, but they were adamant that I had got the wrong day, so I asked when it could be rearranged for.

"It's too late for that I'm afraid. We had to let them go without charge."

I couldn't believe what I was hearing but knew it would be futile to argue. I wonder how much worse the attack would have been if there had been nobody else around, or if there had been something lying around that they could have used as a makeshift weapon. The group who attacked me seemed to have no concern whatsoever about their actions, and it could easily have been a lot worse than it was. It could easily have been Lloyd who had been called in the middle of the night to be told that I had been killed, and not the other way round. The way the whole thing was handled made it hard for me to trust the police at the time.

It wasn't me who had been killed, though, it was Lloyd, and now I was about to head through town as part of his funeral procession. I was grateful at the effort the undertakers had gone to in order to make Lloyd look more like himself, and in the hearse there was a huge floral "Lloyd" in tribute to him, which was a nice touch. We had been asked if we wanted to go through town following the hearse or to take a longer but quieter route. We said we didn't mind either way, but that we might as well go through town. It was one of the strangest experiences I think I will ever have. We were following my brother, who was dead in a coffin, through the town I knew so well, and people were just going about their daily lives as if nothing had happened. I wasn't expecting everyone to stop what they were doing and form a guard of honour or anything like that, but all the same, the case had been all over the news, and so I was a little surprised when we only saw one person tip their hat during the whole journey. Everyone seemed oblivious as we drove my brother towards the flames of the crematorium. I was later able to reflect that just because there were no outward signs of peoples' acknowledgement doesn't mean that nobody cared. I thought about how I never usually stop when I see a hearse go by, although my thoughts are with the family of the deceased.

We arrived at the gates of the crematorium and stopped to get out of the car. The RAF had arranged for a fly-past, which would signify the beginning of a minute's silence in the town centre. We seemed to be waiting for hours, but eventually the deafening roar of the jet engines filled the sky. Lloyd's death had a huge impact on the cadets, and they were all lining the driveway towards the doors of the building where the funeral would take place. I felt a surge of pride that all of these young people in uniform had gathered to pay tribute to my brother. This provided a momentary respite from my fears about dropping the coffin. The funeral director had assured me this wouldn't happen, but then he wouldn't exactly say "yes, you will definitely drop the coffin" would he?

When we reached the doors, the hearse stopped and the moment I had been dreading had arrived. It would be myself, my uncles, and my dad who would carry the coffin and we all had to put padded drapes on our shoulders to help us. They lowered the coffin onto our shoulders, which seemed to take forever, and then when it finally settled, I thought "Bloody hell, Lloyd—you're heavy!" Luckily, I didn't think it aloud.

We walked in and carried the coffin to the front, but I don't remember putting it down or finding my way to my seat. Lloyd's iPod had been plugged into the speakers and a selection of his favourite songs were playing to the hundreds of people in attendance. There were over a thousand people altogether, but not all of them could fit in the room and so quite a few were gathered outside as well, despite the torrential rain that seemed to have set in for the day. People just continued to stand respectfully outside during the service, even though they were probably drenched, which really meant a lot to me. They barely seemed to flinch as the rain hammered down. I remember a few specific songs that all took on an extra poignant meaning under the circumstances. "Drive" by Incubus, with its chorus that reassures of one's steadfast presence through all of life's tribulations, just made me think of all the future events Lloyd would not be there for. "Stop Crying Your Heart Out" by Oasis was one of his absolute favourites, and he had made a video with some of his friends of them driving to the beach and listening to that song. "Wake Me Up When September Ends" by Green Day simply because it was September when he died.

Our local village vicar, who had known Lloyd since he was very young, took the service. I remember him speaking of how the rain symbolised the angels weeping for the loss of Lloyd from the world. I found this touching at the time and always have since. I can remember little of my own speech, which it was important for me to make even though I had no idea what to say. I looked for a friendly face amid the sea of people and picked out my partner, Ben, almost straight away. He appeared calm and composed in total contrast to my family, who were obviously distraught, and it was very helpful to see somebody I knew who was able to remain composed at the time. I know I told everyone how proud I was to have Lloyd as a brother but beyond that, I can't remember a thing.

At the end of the service, each member of our family approached the front with a single red rose, which we placed on top of the coffin. We said our final goodbyes and then it was time to leave him and talk to the guests, who we were so grateful had joined us to say goodbye. I remember talking to one of my old primary school teachers, who seemed quite distracted at the time, but it would have been natural for people to feel awkward and not really know what to say to me. It was the strangest day of my life, from when we got to the Funeral Directors until the end of the service and beyond. The service had all gone very smoothly, and I felt a little guilty because on such a sad day I had really enjoyed catching up with some old friends I had not seen for a long time.

At the wake I didn't feel like being in the main room, and so myself, Ben, and some close friends hung out together in a side room and shared some of our favourite memories of Lloyd. My friends were going out that night and they asked if I wanted to come. I wasn't sure if it would be appropriate, but I was definitely glad of the company and so I said yes. We headed straight into town so were still in our smart clothes, and I ended up bumping into a lot more old friends, including one who had lost his father a few years ago. We were able to talk about loss, and he said if I ever wanted to meet up somewhere a little quieter to talk things through properly, he would be more than happy to.

My social life was more active than it had been for quite some time, possibly ever. More old friends got in touch and invited me out. I realised that this probably wouldn't have happened if it wasn't for the situation I was in, but I wasn't bothered about anyone's motives; I was just really glad of the company, and the chance to talk about Lloyd in a positive way through happy memories. I would be out more often than not at first, and Ben even said he was concerned about me becoming an alcoholic at one point. I have always been able to control my drinking, I was just trying to get through an awful situation the best I could. It was only social drinking, and I wasn't really drinking to get drunk. We would meet in quiet pubs in town and have a few drinks rather than hitting a packed nightclub and downing shot after shot.

I remember the night of the carnival we went to the pub and every drink was a toast "to Lloyd," as was some candyfloss we ate. There was plenty of laughter, but obviously there was still a huge amount of sadness just beneath the surface, which threatened to erupt at any point. Several times I would go from howling with laughter to feeling like I was about to burst into tears, but I would always stop myself. I wanted to remember Lloyd in a happy way and didn't want to bring the atmosphere down, although I'm sure people would have understood if I became emotional.

Of course, the threat of violence was always in the back of my mind. I knew that it was a real possibility if you were in the wrong place at the wrong time, just as Lloyd had been and just as I had been not long before. On one night out I was trying to light a cigarette when a group of lads walked towards us and I remember thinking "Don't catch their eye! Don't catch their eye!" I accidentally made eye contact with one of the group and braced myself for the worst, the panic probably being evident all over my face, then they walked past. I breathed a huge sigh of relief, then I almost gasped as one of the group reappeared next to me. I was wondering whether I should run and was absolutely terrified.

"Do you want a light, mate?" he smiled, and that was that. There were no more incidents. Because I was so young, I was lucky to have a lot of friends who didn't yet have many responsibilities in life, and so they were able to join me frequently on nights out. It must have been extremely hard for my parents to get through those times, even though they could count on support from the rest of the family. What I didn't like was how some people tried to gain attention from pretending they had some kind of connection to Lloyd. Once at Uni I overheard someone who had the same surname but from a different family saying "yeah, he was my cousin" and lapping up the resultant attention. I couldn't believe it really, but I didn't go over and say anything. What was the point?

Despite the happy times I shared with friends, I was full of grief for the brother I had lost, and during any quiet moments, the numbness would hit me again. The next thing we would all have to go through as a family would be the trial of those who attacked him. I knew little about them at the time, and although I had some negative experiences with the police on other occasions, they always did a good job of keeping us informed when it came to Lloyd's case. His attackers were picked up at dawn the day after he died; some of them had been thrown out of several pubs in town on the day and the police put two and two together, making four on this occasion. A couple of the lads already had ASBOs, and they were known to the police for fights and anti-social behaviour they had been involved in on previous occasions.

The car that pulled up when Lloyd had been attacked, causing his attackers to run, was driven by one of the parents of someone who had been at the party he was at. Who knows what else might have happened had they not arrived when they did? Would Lloyd have been the only one who had died? There will always be questions about that night that can't be answered. What we do know is that Lloyd and several of his friends had been at a party at the new hockey club in Staplegrove and had offered to stay behind to help clear up. Had they left straight away and not offered to help would they have come across the group who attacked them? We know that they met the group walking the other way and one of them attacked one of Lloyd's friends, who managed to break free, but then they were chased, and Lloyd was the slowest to run away, so he took the worst of the attack. We will probably never know whether the one who struck him with a wooden sign intended to kill him, because to this day he denies even remembering the incident, but during the trial we would hear in graphic detail what they had done. I truly would not wish it upon anyone, and if I have since helped to prevent it happening to one other person, let alone a number of others, I will consider my life to have been a success.

A Traumatic Three Weeks

I have heard some horror stories over the years from bereaved parents about the way the police have dealt with them, but I can't fault our family liaison officers in the way they supported us or managed the case every step of the way. They kept us informed right from the start and treated us with kindness and compassion. We were lucky to be assigned officers who took on the role because they genuinely wanted to make a difference, and their care for the families they were assigned to support came from a place of true understanding.

The trial didn't begin for almost a year after Lloyd died; murder cases are often very complex and it takes time to gather evidence, interview witnesses, and prepare for what is of course a very serious trial. My family would meet the liaison officers at the local supermarket car park, and they would drive us to and from the court each day.

I do not necessarily believe in God, but I have always believed that there are some things you cannot explain with science and that there is definitely a spiritual dimension to life. Several things happened during the trial that even made both my resolutely non-believing dad and partner question things. My dad woke up on the day of the trial with the song "Don't Worry, Be Happy" in his head and tried to drown it out because it seemed so inappropriate. He mentioned it to us on the way to court, wondering why today of all days that song would be the one he would wake up hearing. No more was said about it until we arrived and were shown to the family waiting room. We didn't want to be where we were, because of the reason we were there, but the room was comfortable, and it helped to take the edge off our nerves. We were chatting a little bit, and suddenly my mum and dad, who were sat opposite me, both laughed as their eye widened and their mouths fell open. I looked round and saw pictures of two of the characters from *Snow White and the Seven Dwarfs* on the wall: Doc and Happy. Underneath the pictures were the words "Don't Worry, be Happy!"

We couldn't believe what we were seeing, and on one of the most difficult days since the funeral, we felt like Lloyd was with us and would help us get through these challenging times. These kinds of coincidences have kept happening over the years; either on Lloyd's birthday or when something makes the thoughts of him re-emerge, that song will come on the radio. It happens with "Wake Me Up When September Ends" by Green Day, too. Neither of these songs are exactly contemporary nowadays, but they still somehow manage to get played on the radio during any poignant time for our family. It's almost like Lloyd somehow phones in from beyond the grave to request them, just to make us feel like he's still with us.

The time came eventually for us to be called into the courtroom. The lighter atmosphere dissipated because I knew I was about to see Lloyd's killers. Three of their group would stand trial: Jay Wall, Andrew Betty, and one of their friends. The latter would be found innocent due to lack of forensic evidence. I had no idea how I would feel to see the men who were responsible for my brother's death. Would I want to yell at them? Would I feel like bursting into tears? Would I be able to remain calm? As it happened, if it hadn't been for the situation, I might have stifled a laugh when I saw them. These brutal killers just looked like "skanky chavs" dressed for show in suits! It just seemed absurd that they were capable of such extreme violence. My mum would later say that they had looked like frightened little kids to her. I tried not to look at them too much, but I noticed from the start that one of the three was visibly nervous. The other two seemed to be full of swagger and looked like they found the whole thing quite ridiculous, but one of the lads' body language told a different story. Over the course of the trial, I would almost feel sorry for him. I would later learn that his name was Jay Wall. The other two, as far as I'm aware, have never shown any remorse for what happened and so I find it hard to think of them as anything but nasty gits! Perhaps they do feel remorse deep down and everything is just a front. We will probably never know, but during the trial I never saw anything to suggest they were sorry for the pain they had caused.

Helen Wilson, who covered the whole of the trial for Somerset County Gazette, shared this feeling. She was used to reporting on a number of court cases, but this was on a different level to anything she had experienced before. She had thought that this kind of violence, although she was aware it did happen, only took place in cities such as Bristol, and was shocked that it had taken place on her doorstep. She recalls looking at Lloyd's killers and finding it so hard to understand how they could be capable of what they did.

"I knew I was at work," she recalls. "And I had to remain professional, but I couldn't help feeling a massive sense of anger and disbelief at what had happened to Lloyd."

She was living in a flat in the centre of Taunton, and before going back there each day, when she had driven back from the court in Exeter, she had to go somewhere else to unwind. Putting into words what she had experienced in court was difficult and intense, and she experienced a degree of insomnia after what she had seen and heard each day. The trial had a profound impact on her, and for the few weeks it took place it became her life, such was her inability to switch off from what was happening.

"Lloyd's murder was definitely the most important event I covered during my eight years as a regional news reporter," she says. "It changed the way I thought of myself as a reporter and my perspective on life. I met Lloyd's family during the trial, and when talking to them, it made me realise exactly the kind of reporter I never wanted to be. I couldn't understand how anyone can hound bereaved families on their doorsteps, and was determined to report everything as accurately, respectfully, and sensitively as possible."

All three of the defendants had entered "not guilty" pleas, which was not unexpected but meant that we weren't spared having to sit in court and listen to what happened to Lloyd in graphic detail. I understood that the prosecution lawyer had to do this in order to help the jury know what they had to make a decision on, but to hear it all out loud was just unbearable. The opening statement is a complete blur when I try to think of it now, but the prosecution described blow by blow what happened. They spoke about how Lloyd had left a party with several of his friends after staying behind to help clear up, and that they came across another group containing the defendants. One of the defendants had started a fight with one of Lloyd's group, who managed to break free, and then they all ran but were pursued by the defendants. Lloyd was the slowest to run away and he took the worst of the attack.

"The defendant picked up a wooden post from the side of the road," began the prosecution lawyer, "and he swung it like an axe, felling Lloyd Fouracre, who did not move again, suggesting that he was unconscious. Despite this, Mr. Fouracre was struck once, possibly twice more while he was on the ground. These blows were intended to cause serious harm and were of such force that pieces of the victim's hair and flesh were embedded in the post."

He was talking about the brother I had grown up with and, despite our disagreements, I had always tried to protect. To hear how quickly and how brutally his life was taken away made me feel like exploding with tears, just as I had when I'd seen his body the first time after the injuries had been inflicted. There was nothing anyone could have done to prevent what happened to him because it is entirely probable that the first blow alone would have been fatal. How could anyone do that to another human being? What was in their head?

"The attack on Mr. Fouracre did not end there," continued the lawyer. "After he had been struck with the sign another of the defendants kicked him in the head like he was a footballer taking a penalty shot. He was kicked and stamped on a number of times."

Before then we had a vague idea of what had happened to Lloyd, but to hear it all in such detail in front of those who committed those despicable acts was just too much. I wanted to run out of the room right there and then, but the door was on the other side of the room, and for me to get out a lot of people would have had to move out of the way. I managed to hold back the tears until recess had been called, and I tried to just stroll out of the court to find a quiet place, but all of the pent-up emotion was rising to the surface with every step. The tears began to build up in my eyes and obscured my vision just as I was getting to the turnstile barrier. Brilliant! The barrier was doing all it could to try and stop me getting through as well, or at least this was how it seemed. I was wrestling with it whilst tears streamed down my face, and I was unable to move. It seemed like forever before I was finally able to make it through, and I ran as fast as I could to get outside where grief just erupted and I couldn't get enough tears out. I could barely breathe, and my whole body was convulsing. I must have looked a right mess, but luckily the first person to come across me was my auntie, who had followed me out. We cried together for a while before I pulled myself together. She had been a wonderful calming presence through all that had happened. She worked at the college where I had been doing my nursing training, so we had been able to have a number of heart-to-hearts on days when I really needed it. She was always someone I could talk to when I felt lonely.

At that point, I knew that no matter how hard the trial got, several of my family were there and we had each other, even if Lloyd was no longer with us. We would get through this time together, even if nothing would ever be the same again. The jury heard over the next couple of days how one of Lloyd's friends had tried to stop the initial attack with the wooden post by grabbing his attacker in a bear hug and trying to wrestle him to the ground, at which point he was attacked himself by some of the others. He had been lucky to escape with only superficial injuries. Others of Lloyd's friends who had been with him that night bravely took the stand and confirmed, in their own words, what the prosecution lawyer had said in his opening statement: that the defendants had intended to cause maximum possible harm. Again, the lads sitting in the dock seemed so at odds with my expectations. They just looked like the kind of kids who might have bullied me at school, but not violent killers who were capable of the level of brutality we were hearing about. I had real trouble getting my head around the fact that these were the ones who had caused my brother's death, and I found it hard to feel too much hatred towards them because it all just seemed so surreal. What kind of society did we live in that boys like these could be vicious killers?

A member of the A&E staff took the stand and told of how they had tried to save Lloyd, but his injuries were just too many and were too severe, and that after just half an hour of him arriving at hospital they were forced to give up trying to resuscitate him. This was also extremely hard to hear, that there had basically been no possibility of saving Lloyd's life. Obviously, it may have been worse to hear that there had been a chance, but they'd failed. It just reinforced how ferocious the attack was, and I kept asking myself "Why?" What did Lloyd do to anyone to deserve that? Why were these young lads so angry, so filled with hatred that they were capable of what they did?

As the days went on, we heard more evidence, and of course there was the defence as well as the prosecution. The defendants didn't give evidence themselves; everything was done through their lawyers, but two claimed not to remember the incident whatsoever, and the third said that he had stood by and watched as the attack took place but had not taken part. We knew that it was all nonsense, and hoped the jury would see it too, but two of the defendants also had character witnesses. One was their auntie and the other was a neighbour, who we suspected may have been threatened into telling the jury what a good lad he had been up until then because the defendant's family were known for that kind of behaviour.

We had little faith in the justice system and knew that the sentences Lloyd's killers received, if they were even found guilty, would seem inadequate. There would be no sense of victory as far as we were concerned if they were handed life sentences. They would be out some day and perhaps able to continue their lives. Lloyd would never be able to. At the time it all seemed so senseless. Whatever happened to these lads, it wouldn't bring

Lloyd back. Of course we did want them to be found guilty, and we didn't want them to have a chance to be back out on the streets and doing the same thing within months.

I did feel sorry for the members of the jury because I noticed a number of them had tears in their eyes when they heard all the details of what had happened. It seemed unfair that they were being dragged into our tragic story, and that they had to play such a key role in the outcome when none of them knew us. They took a week to decide on the verdict, and this was by far one of the worst weeks of my life. It must have been difficult for the jury because not only were they deciding our fate, and whether we would have felt we had any kind of justice for our lost loved one, but the fate of three young lads who had families of their own. A number of the jury may well have been parents themselves, and they had not known any of us before the trial. They had to make a decision purely based on everything they'd heard, from both sides.

We had to come back to court each day during that week, just in case "today was the day," and each time it was equally draining. We would go to bed feeling anxious about the next day yet exhausted from the day that had just come to an end, and when we woke up all of the anxieties would come straight back. Would this be the day the ordeal of the trial was over? What would the verdict be? What would happen next? How would we try and move on with our lives?

There was a lot of waiting, and every day dragged on like I'd never known. There was the feeling of anticipation that we could be called in at any moment to hear the verdict, but that moment never came, and it was really quite exhausting. I have heard since that a week is a long time for a jury to come to a decision and is quite rare. We will never know what they talked about during that week, but it must have been very tiring for them as well.

Helen, the journalist, remembers desperately hoping that the defendants would be found guilty and that they would go to prison for a long time. She found it so hard to get her head round the fact that young people like them were capable of such brutal violence, and she knew it was important that their punishment reflected the damage they had caused. She had built up a good relationship with the police during the trial, and later became a press officer for Avon and Somerset Police. When anyone mentions Lloyd now, she is taken right back to those days and has never forgotten how she felt during the trial.

"I felt a sense of responsibility to Lloyd's family at the time to do a good job of reporting what happened, and to make sure people knew what they had gone through," she explains. "I have often thought about them since, and really hoped they were able to find a degree of peace and to move on with their lives in some way. I really admire Adam for the campaigning work he has done, and I wish him the very best."

Finally, at the end of the longest week of my life, came the moment we had been waiting for. We were called in to the courtroom, and again what was said is a total blur, but I remember the looks on various peoples' faces most of all. One of the defendants was stood in the dock like he was king of the world. He seemed completely untroubled and even looked proud of himself. Another looked like he wasn't really sure what was going on and was just staring into space as if his mind was on something else. The third, Jay, looked absolutely terrified. He was visibly trembling and was the only one of the three who seemed remorseful. I wasn't sure if he was afraid of what was going to happen to him, was coming to terms with what he had done, or was feeling sorry, but I did feel a degree of sympathy. For the other two, I felt nothing.

The guy who seemed distracted was found not guilty due to a lack of forensic evidence. I must admit there did seem to be an over-reliance on forensics. I'm sure this is common these days with such advances in tech and the need for certainty, but multiple verbal accounts given in court by the defendants' friends all tell the same story, that he was involved and had washed blood from the bicycle seat he used as a weapon. Police retrieved a soaking bicycle seat with no blood. No blood equals no forensics despite the stories adding up. Of course this was not the outcome we wanted, but it was not entirely unexpected. He had also been allowed a character reference whilst Lloyd was not, and from what we had heard he'd not been one of the instigators of the attack. My personal belief is that he joined in, and was at least partly responsible, but this was not what the court decided, and so he walked free. We understand that he went on to commit other acts of violence since the trial, but thankfully no more lives have been lost as a result of these.

The other two didn't get off so lightly. The head of the jury was sobbing as she read out the verdict, through which Andrew Betty and Jay Wall were convicted of murder. Andrew smirked as the verdict was read out, Jay looked horrified. I don't know if that smirk was just bravado, but whether it was or not, it must take a cold heart to act that way in front of the family of a young man whose death you were responsible for. I made very little eye contact with any of the defendants during the trial, and I didn't particularly want to. We were also told not to, as it could prejudice the trial. We felt like anything we did wrong could have this impact; we were living on tenterhooks. I felt very little when the verdict was read out. If the lad who had killed Lloyd thought of it all as a big joke, then would it really make a difference what the judge was about to say?

Jay: Three

Loyalty is a strange thing. Most lads would probably agree that when you're young and have a group of close friends you say you'll have each other's backs no matter what. It feels like this is true. I wonder, though, how many would remain loyal if it was truly tested. This was exactly what happened to our group in September 2005. We were being charged with murder, and at first, we planned to say nothing, but after a couple of days of police interviews, it went from "all for one and one for all" to "every man for himself" very quickly.

I was taken straight to the police station after being arrested at home, and when I first got there, I felt scared. Over the course of a few days, I probably told them four different accounts of what had happened, none of them being true. I just wanted to say anything apart from what I'd actually done because I still didn't want to face up to it. When we first got arrested, we agreed not to say anything, because of the idea of not being a grass and of loyalty to each other, but this went out of the window when we began to realise what the consequences would be. I remember when I went to my first interview, I was told various things about what different people had said, and over time I realised that the loyalty we pretended to have to each other meant nothing. The only people who will really be there for you when you need them are your loved ones.

After a couple of days of interviews, it was all about self-preservation. I remember hearing some things said about what I'd done that had never actually happened, and I don't know what my co-defendants said, but I never held a grudge against any of them for what lies they may or may not have told about me. I did the same. Although there was always potential for us to end up in trouble, I'm not sure any of us actually ever thought we would be in such a serious situation, and so we had no idea how to deal with it.

It wasn't until the fifth day of interviews that someone came to formally charge us. We were in our own individual cells, and I remember the police officer coming to mine.

"Am I going home?" I asked him, genuinely believing this was what would happen.

"You're not going anywhere, mate," he replied without emotion. "You're going to prison."

I was stunned and got quite upset. Prison was never somewhere I had wanted to go. There was a certain status symbol for some of the people I hung out with around having done time, but I just felt scared. There was no display of bravado, no front, I just let the police officer see exactly how scared I was.

"How long am I going to prison for?" I said.

"Until the trial. You'll be standing trial for the murder of Lloyd Fouracre."

"What?"

I knew at this point that someone had died because of me, but I just don't think it had sunk in what it would mean. I had some festering anger because of some things I'd been through in life, and through venting that anger somebody had lost their life. At that point in the police cell, I still couldn't have looked in the mirror and said, "Lloyd died because of me." I was still quite blinkered, and I just didn't want to admit to myself that I was responsible for that. How could I process it?

When I was 16 or 17, which was only a few years before I went to prison, if someone had sat me down and said, "You're going to kill someone," I would have told them "you're crazy." The thought of being responsible for someone's death just never entered my head. It was something that other people did; much nastier people than me. I didn't even think of myself as a bad person. I could imagine being in a fight and hurting someone. Of course I hoped that if I fought anyone, I would come off best, but did I ever imagine I'd have to kill somebody for that to happen, or that it might happen by accident? No way; of course not. Not many people would fight if they thought someone was gonna die because of it. Only people with no guilt, no remorse, no regard for someone else's life. That was definitely not who I was, even back then.

I didn't know anything about Lloyd or his family at this point. I didn't know he had a brother; I didn't know what he had done with his life. I hadn't seen him as a person with a family who loved him when I went over to start a fight with his friends. He could have been literally anyone, and that's maybe one of the scariest things about it. I knew absolutely nothing about him, but I didn't care. I just saw him as a punchbag to take my frustration out on. Anyone I'd seen who happened to be walking by at that moment would have been the same.

Yeah, my pride had been hurt after the scuffle with John. Yeah, I was angry with my mates for mugging me off in front of the girl earlier in the night, but those things don't make the average person go up to a total stranger and start swinging for them. I had anger that had been building up in me over years, and it started when I was very young. There were reasons for my actions, and I will explain what they were, but none of those reasons excuse the fact that I was responsible for an innocent young man losing his life. It was right that I went to prison. I didn't think so at the time though. In the moment I was just scared for myself and had no real regard for any of the people who were hurt by what I had done. It took time to make me realise the impact my actions had. Back in September 2005 as I sat in that police station being told I was going to prison I was just terrified.

The Verdict

Thursday 3rd August 2006 was the day Lloyd's killers received their sentences. As Judge Cottle gave his closing statement I felt quite relieved that the trial was over, but other than that I just felt quite numb. I'm not sure his words truly sank in, but I tried to listen.

"Andrew Betty and Jay Wall," he began. "You have both been convicted by this jury of the murder of Lloyd Fouracre, and the sentence that is passed upon you is one of custody for life."

I knew that "life" did not mean that at all. These young lads would be out of prison while they were still quite young. The judge said himself that they would serve a minimum term before their release would be considered and that a risk assessment would be taken before the parole board made their decision. It seemed likely that they would be out in much less time than seemed fair, considering that their actions had robbed Lloyd of his future.

"The court and the jury have spent three weeks listening to an all-too-familiar story of young men fuelled by alcohol resorting to completely unprovoked and extreme violence. In that violence, a young life was lost. It was needlessly lost, and needlessly and brutally taken."

This I did agree with, and it seemed that the judge was confirming my assertion that violence was a huge problem in our society. He continued.

"It is far from clear what triggered this outbreak of violence. It seems to be the case, in this rapidly deteriorating society in which we live, that this sort of incident has become endemic. No excuse or provocation is required as justification for violence, and all that the courts can do in attempting, I suspect unsuccessfully, to stem the tide is to hand down sentences that reflect the view of the law-abiding public towards this increasing social problem. Both of you had drunk huge quantities of alcohol. You, Betty, on your own admission, had been drinking all day, and of the two of you, you must be the one who takes a greater share of responsibility for what occurred."

So what the judge was essentially telling us was that he believed any punishment he could hand out would be futile and that he believed that violence was an inevitable part of life going forward. This could not be right, although again it did confirm what I had been thinking when reflecting on the problem of violence as a whole. It was a major problem, and something had to be done.

"By the time you left the Staplegrove Public House it was almost inevitable that something was going to happen, and until you could find somebody else to fight you fought between yourselves. The prospect of you passing Lloyd Fouracre's well-behaved group as they left that 18th birthday party—the prospect of you passing them without resorting to violence was non-existent. You, Betty, initiated the violence by inflicting two extremely heavy blows with the disabled parking sign. The first felled Lloyd. He never moved after that. Notwithstanding that, you struck him a second blow and were about to strike him for a third time when Zach Osborne grabbed you and pulled you away. I have little doubt that had that not happened you would have continued to strike him. I make it clear I do not accept that you cannot recall what you did. What I would accept is that you are so horrified by the recollection of it that you would rather pretend that you cannot recall it."

There is only one person who knows for sure what is true, and at the time of writing, I have not heard anything to suggest he will ever tell me. I don't particularly want to meet Andrew, as I have never been told he has shown a shred of remorse for what happened, but not knowing why he did what he did is something that will always make it difficult to have closure. Hearing again about the brutality of his actions was hard, and it isn't something I could ever imagine myself doing, even with provocation. Why does anyone display that level of violence for no apparent reason?

"You, Wall, as Lloyd lay motionless, unconscious and grievously injured, then proceeded to kick him, and that is the only explanation for the blood spattering on your jeans. Lloyd died from horrendous head injuries—injuries caused by blows, by kicks, and by stamps."

I agreed and even hoped that it was the blow with the wooden sign that had knocked Lloyd unconscious and that he felt nothing afterwards. Having said that, I knew that Andrew was not the only one who had carried out extreme violence on him. I'm not sure how many people struck Lloyd, but it seemed obvious that Jay had played a significant part. He looked truly shaken.

"The starting point for the minimum term in relation to both of you is one of 15 years. I am required to consider if there are any circumstances of the case that aggravate, and therefore increase the starting point, and equally whether there are any mitigating features to reduce the sentence below that starting point. The potential aggravating features are set out in Schedule 21, and I find that there are no aggravating features that apply to the case of either of you. As to mitigation, clearly, there are two. Firstly, that this was not a premeditated attack—it was a spontaneous attack; and secondly, I am required to take into account, and I do, the age of each one of you."

At this point, it seemed inevitable that they would receive a sentence that would seem woefully inadequate. Fifteen years had been mentioned, but I wasn't quite sure what this meant. Would this be the length of their sentence? Was it a minimum? Was it a maximum? The last bit of his statement had sounded like legal jargon and I had not really taken a lot of it in. He had said he would be taking their age into account. Did this mean they would only be in prison for a few years?

"The effect of the events of that night upon those near and dear to Lloyd is immense. I have not previously read another witness statement which in nearly every sentence so graphically describes the dreadful numbing pain that Mr. and Mrs. Fouracre and their family experience every waking moment. Their son was a thoroughly decent young man who promised so much, and he was a son of whom they were justly proud."

I recalled the complete shock I had felt when my dad had first called me in the middle of the night to tell me what had happened. I had been unable to take it in, and in a way, I still couldn't. It would have been enough of a shock if Lloyd had died in a car accident, or had a sudden brain haemorrhage as his friend had, but that his life had been taken from him by another lad of a similar age? It all seemed so unfair, and I was not sure I would ever truly wrap my head around it.

"Taking into account the mitigating features, I have decided that the minimum terms will be in your case, Betty, 13 years and in your case, Wall, 12 years. The minimum term means exactly what it says. It is not the period that you will serve; it is the period that you will serve before any consideration is given to releasing you back into the community, and your release will depend entirely upon an assessment by the parole board that your risk has been reduced to a level that can be properly and safely managed in the community. Until that day arrives you will remain in custody. In relation to those terms of 13 years and 12 years, the time spent in custody by both of you will be taken into account, and the order for imprisonment will reflect that you both spent 309 days in custody."

I remember feeling no change in emotion when the length of the jail term was read out, but after a quick calculation in my head I figured out that they would most likely be out of prison by the time they were in their early 30s. This felt like nowhere near long enough, but the only thing that could really make up for what they had done was impossible. They could not bring Lloyd back, or turn back the clock to prevent what they had done from ever having taken place. The reality was that the world would never again have Lloyd as a part of it, and nothing the judge could have said would change that. When a life is taken, nothing can be done to make it better. At least Jay seemed to feel a degree of remorse. When the judge called for them to be taken down his head was bowed, whilst Andrew swaggered out of there like a rock star.

It was not even a year yet since Lloyd had died, but it seemed like so much more time had passed. Now the funeral was quite a long way behind us and the trial had been and gone, it was time to look to the future, but what kind of future was there after such a horrific loss? The lads who were responsible would be back on the street in just over a decade, and who was to say they would have changed? They might be responsible for another death someday. They might be in and out of prison their whole lives. How many more families would be torn apart? How many more lives would be lost?

These were the questions that were going round in my head before the trial, but afterwards, they only intensified. I knew that it would take me a long time to come to terms with what had happened, and I wasn't sure I ever would. I was so young, and I still had my whole life ahead of me, but what did anything mean now? I was desperate for Lloyd's death not to have been in vain, but where would I even begin when trying to do something about it? As it turned out, I was already on the path.

Jay: Four

We were on remand for nearly a year before the trial began, but even when it was going on, I could never have imagined what the judge was going to say at the end. If someone had said to me "you'll be found guilty and you'll spend over ten years in prison" I would have said, "No way." That was my response to it all. No way. There had to be some kind of mistake. There had to be a way to turn back the clock so none of this had happened. I never meant to kill anyone, so surely I wouldn't be found guilty of murder. It would be manslaughter at the very worst. Might even be accidental death and I would just get a suspended sentence or probation? Could that happen? I wasn't gonna spend the whole of my twenties in prison. No way, no way, no way!

That was exactly what happened though. I'd been shaking in the dock when the jury said they found me guilty, and I was waiting for the judge to tell me the length of my sentence. I was scared of going to prison. A proper jail, not a remand centre, which is bad enough. How long would I be there for? How would I get through it? When the judge said twelve years, I just couldn't believe it. My mouth was dry. My heart was hammering in my chest. I couldn't stop shaking. It was only a year ago I'd been spending my free time playing football, hanging out with friends, just living the life of a normal teenager really. Now I would have a whole lot more free time but a lot less choice over what I did with it.

Prison is really not a good place to be. There are people in there who, as in any walk of life, are going to be the way they will be. They will come out of there exactly the same as they went in and will probably just go back and live the same life they were living before. I think if you go into prison and want to change you can, but you have to really want to. If the strong desire to change isn't there it won't make any difference to your life.

My desire to change came early on. At first, it was because I never wanted to come back to prison again once I was out. It was a number of years before I was able to truly admit to myself that I had belonged in there. When some of the other younger prisoners heard that I was a "lifer" there was a certain amount of kudos that went along with it, and I knew that wasn't the way I wanted to gain respect. I knew from the start that my outlook was very different to a lot of the other inmates.

I never really thought about Lloyd's family in the beginning. It was partly a coping mechanism because I was going to be in there for a long time, and I had to just try and take each day as it came, getting through them one by one. I tried not to think too much about what I'd done, what my actions had caused, and who it had an impact on. I couldn't. I wasn't ready to admit it.

My own family still came to visit me, knowing I had done a really awful thing. They even came to see me in Preston, at the other end of the country. That was when I learnt that your loved ones are the only ones you can ever truly rely on. They're the ones you will always have a connection with no matter what. My upbringing had not been perfect, and some of it had been quite messed up if I tell you the truth, but none of it was my mum's fault. I had opportunities to make something of my life before my actions put me in prison. I could have gone a different way; there was nothing inevitable about me ending up in here. I made choices, and they were the wrong ones. Would I have made them if my dad had been around and I'd had more guidance? Who knows? I can't blame any of what happened on anyone, or anything else apart from the choice I made to start a fight.

All of those considerations would come later though. At the beginning, prison was about survival. I don't know if the fact I'd killed someone made the others a bit wary of me, but I never really got into any fights, and I didn't want to. If you appear weak in there you will have problems, but if you keep up your front and don't go looking for trouble you can generally stay away from it. At least that was my experience.

I tried to find things to do in there, and there wasn't much football to be played so I spent plenty of time in the gym. I would get more and more into it the longer I spent there, and it would become quite a big part of my life, but I wasn't thinking too far ahead at the beginning. I have to admit I met some really cool people in prison; people who wanted to change. Some people in there really weren't good people, though, and were just going to keep on being who they were because they saw nothing wrong with it. It's pretty scary that people don't see a problem with being violent for no reason.

That was the only reason I was able to change—because I knew the difference between right and wrong from an early age. You can know what is the right decision to make but still choose to do the opposite. In the end, I wanted to make the right decisions. I just wish I'd made them a lot sooner. I would have saved a huge amount of suffering, and I don't just mean for Lloyd's family.

Of course, none of this has been easy on my family either. My home was already broken before any of this, so I didn't break it through my actions, but my mum moved out of Taunton soon after the trial and I know my brother had a hard time at school because of what happened. My relationship with my brothers wasn't great, but they never got any guidance from me, and without a dad around they were probably relying on me to be a male role model. My youngest brother went off the rails and started smoking weed and doing the things that I was doing. I have another brother who was around Lloyd's age, in fact Lloyd might even have been at Ladymead School when I was there.

I thought a lot more about my family over the years I was inside, and later on, I thought about Lloyd's family a lot more. It seems crazy how one bad decision could have caused everything it did, but that's the truth, and nothing will ever change that. I had a lot of time to think about the mistake I'd made. I made a truly awful decision and caused more pain to more people than I can bear to think about. I deserved to be in prison; I can say that now with absolute certainty.

Starting a Legacy

After the trial ended and two of Lloyd's attackers had begun their prison sentences the media interest began to subside. Up until then, the case was appearing everywhere, in the papers and on TV news reports, both locally and nationally. This was around the time that ASBOs, "hoodies" and "chavs" were all over the news and the idea of delinquent youths causing trouble on the streets was very much at the forefront of peoples' minds. What happened to Lloyd was symptomatic of the issue of a culture of violence among some young people, which may have been hyped in the media but was most definitely a problem in our country and still is to this day. The stereotypes may well play into the issue because a young person wearing a tracksuit may instil fear just because they have the image of the typical violent young thug you see on the news. However, according to the Office of National Statistics (2018), someone under the age of 26 is more likely than other age groups to be either the victim or perpetrator of a violent assault.

Once the news reports moved on to the next story life began to return to some kind of normality, but of course nothing was the same. The elephant in the room at every family gathering was that Lloyd was not with us. Our once close and happy family unit would never be the same again because a key part of the unit was missing and could never be replaced. Special occasions that were once a time for celebration now just amplified the tragedy that had torn our family apart. The joyful family Christmases we had once shared were no more, and there was a gaping void in all of our lives.

I knew that my grief over Lloyd's senseless death would never completely go away, and so I knew that I had to try and do something to try and stop it from happening to someone else. The idea for Stand Against Violence had already come about in around November 2005 when I was sat with a friend at my parents' house. She said the simple sentence "Something needs to be done to try and stop something like this happening again." It was as if a lightbulb switched on in my brain.

"You're right," I said. "We do need to do something to try and stop this from happening again!"

Of course at this early stage, we had no idea what that might be, but I got some pens and paper and we started designing logos. There was the spark of an idea, and sometimes that, coupled with the right amount of enthusiasm and drive, is all it takes to get something started. I have always been passionate about speaking up against the problems I see in our society, perhaps this came from when I was bullied as a child, but I was determined to prevent at least one family from going through what mine had suffered. I thought it might be good to speak to the local police to begin with, and the response was positive at first. I was invited to go out on patrol with a couple of the local officers in town on a Friday night. I accepted the invitation with interest; who gets to do that? I remember we were just cruising through the town when suddenly we saw two groups of lads squaring up to each other. The officers pulled over and got out, quickly defusing the situation and sending the groups off, making sure they went in different directions. Just a quick intervention and that was it; no fight had taken place.

It seemed obvious to me straight away what needed to be done. We needed more of a police presence on the street on Friday and Saturday nights. This is when most violent incidents take place, purely due to a lot more people being out drinking and so more potential for flashpoints. At first, the police had seemed really keen to help me and wanted me to work closely with them, but as soon as I mentioned the idea of a petition to get more police on the streets their whole energy changed. I would soon find out their concern was that doing a petition would make the whole thing political, which they would not be able to support. I was not deterred, and having watched from the passenger seat how quickly and efficiently they had dealt with a potentially violent incident, it seemed so obvious to me that more of a police presence on the streets would help. I was baffled at first as to why they would oppose something that would seemingly help the situation, but I would learn over time that such decisions are always more complex than I would want them to be and that the opposition often comes from individuals in a position of power who have an agenda.

Either way, I quickly weighed up the pros and cons and decided to press on with the petition with or without the support of the local police. I went first to various family members and friends who I knew would support me. I decided it was important to organise a meeting in order to set out what we were actually hoping to achieve and to plan how we would manage it. A friend whose parents ran a local pub allowed us to use their conference room, and once it became real, I started to get nervous. I had spoken to a large crowd at the funeral recently, and most of the people I would be addressing at the meeting would have been there, but this seemed different. At the funeral it wouldn't have mattered much what I had said—I would still have had everyone's support without question. Now I had to set out the mission statement of a campaign that I still wasn't really sure how to get off the ground. I was afraid of sounding stupid, and of people having no confidence in what I was suggesting. I had enjoyed drama lessons at school but talking in front of a crowd just wasn't my thing. If I'd known then the size of the crowds I would address in the future, I would have quaked with fear!

The confidence issues that had their root in my experiences at school were rearing their ugly head, but at the same time, I felt inspired by the number of people who had come to hear what I had to say. My housemate came along for moral support, and some of the people were friends and family of mine, but a lot of them I didn't know. They were mostly friends of Lloyd's who were keen to help ensure his death was not in vain, and to continue to support him in any way they could even though he was no longer here in person. I had not prepared a speech. There was no script, not even any notes. I just told everyone about the petition, how I had seen first-hand the effectiveness of a police presence in preventing violence, and that I was going to petition the government to get more police on the streets on Friday and Saturday nights, which I believed would act as a significant deterrent. I explained that my plan was initially to have teams collecting signatures in town, and pretty much everyone there was willing to help. They all seemed to think it was a good idea, which was such a relief.

The editor of the local newspaper showed a lot of interest to begin with and offered to professionally produce the logo as well as print new petitions when they were needed. To have the media on side was a boost, especially as these were the days before Facebook, so word of mouth and printed media were vital in reaching an audience. The timing for collecting signatures also seemed perfect because it was approaching Christmas and town would be packed. I had already been canvassing a little myself. This didn't always go down well; I tried to get some people to sign at a house party I went to in Cardiff, which they did, but I think the party organisers saw me as "Captain Bringdown." I suppose people usually go to parties to try and forget about the difficult things in life and to let off steam, so I wasn't exactly creating the right vibe by talking about my brother's murder.

This wasn't the only time we received a less than positive response. The petition I had produced had room for 50 signatures per page, and the one the newspaper editor did for us had room for just 15, so we ran out pretty quickly. I mentioned this to him, but he insisted that 15 per page was a good number. He was very happy to print off more for us when we first ran out, and so I went back to him a second time expecting him to be pleased that the campaign was going so well.

"Again?" he said, which took me a little by surprise. "We've printed off quite a few of these for you. This will be the last batch!"

I wasn't quite sure what to say. He seemed genuinely angry, and this just seemed bizarre because we'd not had to plead with him at the beginning; he had come to us, and up until that point he couldn't do enough to help. I wonder if maybe he hadn't expected us to do so well and was thinking he would make a kind gesture but then he could move on to the next story. In any case, we went to a local Staples store for the printing from then on, and it did cost us a fair bit of money as time went on. This was good because it meant we were collecting a lot of signatures, but at the same time I was basically funding everything myself with a little help from my family. We had some t-shirts printed as well, so costs were beginning to mount up. Of course I didn't mind spending money on the campaign because it was so close to my heart, but I had to think in practical terms. I was definitely not rich, and so this was something I would have to consider going forward.

Many of the negative responses we received were from the older generation, which surprised me as I was always hearing about "the youth of today" being responsible for anti-social behaviour. Here we were, some young people trying to make a positive change, but a lot of older people treated us like we were a nuisance. I realise that sometimes people in the street with clipboards are people you want to avoid when you're having a busy day, but it was frustrating and disappointing that more people wouldn't engage with us when the story was all over the media and we had the t-shirts, so it was obvious what we were there to talk about. At times it made me feel disillusioned, but often just when it was starting to really grind me down, I would be approached by someone who would remind me why I was doing all of this, and it would renew my energy and enthusiasm for the campaign.

One lady in particular stands out in my memory. She sought me out specially and told me how she had lost her sister at a young age, and that she really admired and supported what we were doing with the campaign. To have this kind of validation from someone who had been through the same thing made me quite emotional, and I had to go behind the nearby hot dog stand so I could compose myself before continuing. A lot of young people would seek us out having heard about the petition and were very keen to help. To look at some of them I would think they would be people who would start fights, but they would talk to us at length about how much they hated violence and would rush over to sign the petition. This was reaffirming to me that you cannot judge a book by its cover, and that many people I would not expect to support the campaign would actually be very keen to, so I should never write anyone off as a potential supporter until I had actually spoken to them.

We did have some very negative experiences as well as positive. One that shook me up was when two of my uncles had been collecting signatures together and they were chased by some aggressive drunken men in broad daylight. The police were called but they never turned up, and so it was lucky that my uncles were able to get away unharmed. The thought of something bad happening to another member of my family because of the campaign was very unsettling. I don't know if those men were genuinely intent on causing harm, but it did make me think. Luckily that incident was memorable in that it was the only one of its kind.

A friend of Lloyd's who worked in a local supermarket was collecting signatures at the checkout one day. She was starting to explain to one customer what the petition was all about and he turned round to her and said, "Well we all have to die someday." We will never know what was going on in his life that would have made him say such a thing, but she was devastated at his response, and it was a cruel thing to say to a young girl who had lost a good friend.

My grandad helped to collect signatures, but he reported back to me one day that he was ashamed to be an OAP because he had received so many negative responses from people of his age. I had been expecting the older generation to be the most kind and most receptive to what we were doing on the whole, but more often than not the opposite was true. There are so many stereotypes in the media, but my experiences from early in the campaign seemed to turn them on their head. When several people in a row had been rude to me, I couldn't help but feel angry, and after they left, I sometimes wished I'd said something like "Well if it's your child it happens to next, you'll understand!" I'm glad I did manage to keep my cool with everyone. To lose it might have diluted the message I was trying to put across, but it was hard some days. Besides, I would genuinely never wish this upon anyone. Having spoken to others who were collecting signatures I know this was a feeling we shared.

One of the most memorable responses of all was from a very well-dressed and well-spoken gentleman who simply said, "What violence?" when we began to tell him about the campaign. It was clear that he was wrapped up in some kind of upper-class money bubble and was blissfully unaware of the problems of "ordinary" people. Either that or he was just trying to pretend it wasn't an issue for whatever reason. Unfortunately, he was not the only one.

Despite the negativity, we had been going for just over a week and had already collected around 26,000 signatures from the people of Taunton and nearby. Our family liaison officers warned us to be careful about the campaign as it may be seen to be influencing the trial. I tried to bear this in mind, but I was determined not to let the momentum we were building go to waste. The number of people who had signed reminded me that more people had been in favour of what we were trying to achieve than not, and this did help to restore our faith in humanity.

I was given a number of opportunities to appear in the local media, but the police were seemingly trying to use this as a chance to derail the campaign after I had decided to go against their advice. In every report, I would talk about what we were trying to achieve with the campaign, and immediately afterwards a police spokesperson would be shown talking about why they believed it to be counterproductive. Not once had I said that I believed the police were doing a bad job, in fact I was suggesting that there should be more police because I had seen them do such an effective job in defusing a potentially violent situation. However, they said that there was not a serious issue with violence in our local area, and I was both scaremongering and harming their reputation.

I knew first-hand that there was a problem with violence in the town, having both experienced it myself and lost my brother in an unprovoked attack. Many people I knew and many more who had signed the petition agreed that it was an issue, and it felt like the police were trying to sweep it under the carpet in order to make it seem like they were in full control.

I just could not understand their logic, as I was trying to help them bolster their force and was saying that we needed the police to tackle this problem, but I was being met with opposition at every opportunity. Of course compared to the trouble spots of a major city such as London or Manchester the amount of violence in Taunton was on a much smaller scale, but to say that there wasn't an issue at all was just exacerbating the problem as far as I could see. If you pretend there's no violence in a place where it clearly happens and people have lost their lives, then how can a solution be found?

I did find a lot more support from my local MP, who fully backed the campaign and even came on the train to London with me to deliver the petition to number 10 Downing Street. I also had fantastic support from the local BBC radio and TV and got to know both the presenters and reporters quite well. One of the radio reporters also came with me to London, as did my mum. I got to experience first-class train travel for the first time and was interviewed about the campaign, which made me feel quite important . . . at least for the 10 minutes I was answering questions, after which we were sent back to the economy class carriage where we belonged.

I hadn't been to London too many times and was really quite anxious about going there. Having grown up in the sleepy villages of Cushuish and Broomfield I was like a country bumpkin making his way to the big city for the first time and I was glad I had company for the journey. I wasn't used to such huge crowds, and I was daunted by the prospect of having to navigate the famous London Underground system.

Paddington Station seemed colossal when we arrived, and everyone seemed to be on fast forward. We had to carry a number of large, heavy boxes full of petitions through the carriage, and I have never forgotten when I caught the eye of a lady I didn't know and she said, "Good luck." I have no idea to this day who she was, or whether she knew anything about what we were doing, but it really helped to put me at ease to hear her kind words at a time when I was plunging into the unknown. We managed to successfully navigate our way to Downing Street, which was quite different to how I expected. It had always looked like quite an ordinary city street when I had seen it on the news, but in fact it's a cul-de-sac with just a few houses and a security checkpoint with armed guards. I guess it made sense for the Prime Minister's residence to be closed off, but this was not what I had been expecting.

The moment came to go through the security scanner and seeing as none of us were carrying anything we shouldn't have been there was no reason to be nervous, but all the same it was a relief when we got through with no issues. I just couldn't wait to get to the door of number 10, where Tony Blair was still the chief resident at the time. We still had a Labour government, and it would be another few years before the Conservatives began their current reign; first in a coalition government with the Liberal Democrats for a short while and then on their own. My heart was in my mouth as we approached the door, and the sense of anticipation was huge as we got closer. I was carrying a huge pile of boxes, all containing petitions, and I couldn't wait to discuss the campaign with Mr. Blair. I was almost as excited, though, if I'm completely honest, about what it would be like inside. What would the décor be? Would there be obvious wealth on display? What kind of cups would the PM drink his tea out of? Our MP knocked on the door and I tried hard to retain my composure.

After what seemed like minutes the door opened and a security guard, best described as ordinary-looking, stood inside.

"Yes? How can I help you?" he said impassively.

"We've come to deliver these petitions to the Prime Minister," said our MP, instantly taking control of the situation. "But can we start from the knock on the door for the media?"

The security guard nodded and closed the door. I did feel a slight sense of anti-climax, but was happy to go with the flow, and was grateful that our MP was taking the lead for now. He knocked again and the door opened to reveal the same security guard standing there. He took the boxes of petitions from me and I was geared up to go in, but he just thanked us in a professional tone and closed the door. That was it.

To this day I have no idea what happened with the results of all of our hard work. All of those hours spent talking to people on the streets. All the negative responses that shook our morale and then the positive responses that made it all seem worthwhile. All of that just for one brief moment at the door of number 10. No indication that our voices had been heard. I had perhaps been naïve to think that Mr. Blair would welcome us in with a cup of tea and a slice of cake and then listen with eyes wide and hands clasped together, nodding his recognition of every one of the points I made, promising to take the message of the campaign to parliament and speaking on the news days later about the measures the government would take to help reduce violence. He was a busy man, our petition was probably one of very many delivered around that time, and he may never have even known that ours existed. Before we arrived, though, I guess I had been hoping for an audience with the PM.

All was not lost yet, as we also had a meeting with a minister at the Home Office. I knew I would actually have a chance to talk about the campaign with him, and it was an opportunity to make sure our message had been delivered. In all the excitement about heading to Downing Street, I had not paid much attention to this visit and actually had no idea who I was meeting. Within minutes of entering the minister's office, it was clear that he was nothing to do with what we were actually trying to achieve. He was something to do with The Olympics, so it wasn't immediately obvious how we could work together, but I still felt like he could have influence if he believed in the campaign, and I hoped he would discuss it with his peers.

We had a brief conversation, during which I did most of the talking, and he gave no indication that he agreed or disagreed with anything I said. I outlined how we had gathered signatures for a petition to get more police on the streets. I explained some other violence prevention ideas we'd had. He listened attentively, or so it seemed, but after a while I had said all there was to say. It didn't feel like an inspiring meeting, and before I knew it, he thanked us for coming and said he would be in touch before my mum and I were shown out of the building.

As we travelled back to Somerset there was none of the buzz in the atmosphere I was hoping for. In fact, the whole mood was pretty flat, although we tried to remain optimistic. We had done what we came here to do, even if we hadn't had the responses we were hoping for. Now it was a waiting game.

Around a week later we received a letter from the minister we had met with. The envelope had a Home Office stamp, and so I tore it open. It was encouraging that he had written to us so quickly. Sadly, my encouragement evaporated within the first paragraph of the letter. The essence of it was "Thank you for coming to see me. Sorry for your loss, but we won't be following up on any of your ideas. We are planning to ban the sale of imitation weapons though. Thanks again and good luck."

I put the letter down and sighed, trying to think of the positives but finding none. Would the lads who attacked Lloyd have thought twice about it if they'd been unable to buy plastic knives or guns beforehand? Furthermore, I've never seen any evidence since that they were even banned. The campaign had seemed to be going better than I could have hoped for with the success of the petitions, and in such a short space of time. How could the momentum have shifted so quickly? I had seen first-hand that a lot of young people hated violence and wanted to do something to stop it, but what could we actually do if those in a position of influence weren't interested in helping? I knew I would continue the campaign, but I was already beginning to wonder if it would have any impact. Was it actually possible to change the situation, or was violence just a reality that people would have to live with? A wave of sadness hit me, and Lloyd's absence came sharply into focus once again.

Challenging the Comfort Zone

After what happened in London, I hit a low patch. Of course I was still grieving for Lloyd and always would be, but the campaign had given me a focus and now I wasn't sure how long it would be able to continue. What real difference could we make? I knew Christmas was going to be a horrible time and was really touched when one of my Uni tutors anticipated this and invited me to spend it with her family. I was actually asked to come into Uni around this time for a meeting with the Head of Year. They could see that I wasn't really coping with my studies after what I'd been through and they were very sympathetic, but they basically said that my only option was to take some time off and come back for the next academic year. I was upset, as I had tried to hold onto my place on the course for so long. It was, again, something that really helped me to have a focus and I was determined to stay with it, but I understood their decision. There were a number of days when I was unable to come in because I was too upset and couldn't face being around other people. In the end, I had just missed too many classes and it would be unrealistic for me to try and catch up. The staff were very supportive, and I will always remember one of my tutors asking me into her office for a chat one day. I poured everything out, which was unusual for me at the time, and we both cried. I finished before she did! This was surprising as she was known for being quite stern, but maybe it was just a front she put on.

I had to tell my work placements what the Uni had decided, and I didn't have to go into much detail as everyone at the hospital knew what had happened with Lloyd. Thinking about it now, it may not have been great confidentiality, but then it's only natural that when something particularly distressing happens in a workplace the staff will have to talk amongst themselves about it. I'd rather they could get it off their chests and be able to function in their jobs than to keep it all inside and potentially make a mistake through stress. In a hospital setting, you don't want any of the staff to be under any more stress than they already are.

In January 2006, I received a letter from Bruce Thompson, the reverend of a local Methodist church, who had heard about the campaign. I just scanned through the letter to begin with, and from what I could gather they were asking me to speak at the launch of an "Anne Frank and You'" exhibition they were organising. I actually felt quite offended that they would ask this of me so soon after Lloyd had been murdered, and I put it away.

If I had read it through properly on that day I may have reacted differently, but I was still feeling quite disillusioned and frustrated over what had happened with the Home Office, and so I was in the wrong frame of mind to consider anything else. Over the next few months, I was struggling to come up with ideas of how to take the campaign forward, and one day I saw the letter sticking out from one of my desk drawers, having completely forgotten about it. I read it through again and saw that Bruce had actually written very sensitively and politely. I felt a little guilty for not having responded but saw that the date of the exhibition was still in the future, and so I got in touch with him and asked him to tell me more about it.

When I understood the aims of the exhibition, I could see that the letter could have given me a boost at a time when it was really needed. The idea was to tell the story of what happened to Anne Frank but linking it to modern-day violence and prejudice and trying to educate people, to try and stop history from repeating itself. The keynote speaker at the launch would be Saranda Bogujevci, a Kosovan refugee Bruce had been working with in a previous role in Manchester. She had faced unimaginable hardship during the recent war in her home country, and sixteen of her family members had been massacred while she somehow survived along with four other children. She was fifteen at the time, and the incident was known as the Podejevo Massacre, being covered in the media worldwide. Bruce told me how he had facilitated Saranda giving talks in a number of schools, aimed at educating young people and changing the world over time to try and stop prejudice. He told me he felt that I could do the same with my story. This was completely in line with my original aims for the campaign, and so I was definitely interested in hearing more. I gulped when I was told that there would be around 300 people at the launch event. Again, I had talked in front of that many people at Lloyd's funeral but that was totally different to addressing an audience of mostly strangers at an organised event. I would feel like there was an expectation on me to give a great talk, whereas at the funeral I had the support of the crowd no matter what I said.

I was filled with anxiety, but I had regular meetings with Bruce leading up to the event and he was always very kind and supportive, which took the edge off my nerves. After the initial panic had worn off, I began to feel quite inspired by the idea of giving a talk, and my creative side emerged as I thought about making it into more of a presentation. I felt that people would respond better if there was some kind of audio-visual display as well as just a guy talking onstage, and so I started to brainstorm ideas. Thinking about the exhibition, I was drawn to Lloyd's memorial web page. Social media had only just begun then, but a webpage had been created where people could post photos, comments, and memories about him. As I looked through them all I began to picture a montage being set to music. To play in the background I chose "Stop Crying Your Heart Out" by Oasis, which of course was one of his favourite songs. The lyrics and overall feel fit the message perfectly. At the beginning of the video, I would ask people to imagine Lloyd was their sibling, their best friend, or another family member, then some of the comments from the web page would be shown, and to finish I would talk a little about what impact his death had had on me and my family.

I thought I had come up with something that would put the message across effectively, but I was shocked when I showed the video to some of my close friends and family and they burst into tears. At this point, the idea came to me to ask some of Lloyd's friends to come along and support me at the event, and maybe to even say a few words. I wasn't sure if this was too much to ask, but I got an overwhelmingly positive response, and they were only too keen to support what I was doing. My family were, understandably, unable to talk in front of an audience with what happened still being so raw, but they did come along to the event and have supported the campaign right from the beginning.

On the day of the launch, I was a bag of nerves and pleaded with some non-specific higher power to let my presentation go well and for me not to screw it up. As the time came for me to begin and I looked out over the sea of people I just couldn't stop shaking. I thought I must look pretty strange to the audience. Everyone was looking right at me and I would have given anything in that moment not to be there, but as always in these situations I reminded myself why I was doing it and so I found the nerve to carry on. Firstly, it was time to play the presentation, and as the lights dimmed, I went and took a seat next to my family.

This was the first time anyone who didn't know me or Lloyd had seen the film, and so I had no idea if it would have the same impact. How could it really? For those I had shown it to so far, there had been an emotional connection. As soon as an image of Lloyd appeared on the screen and the music was playing my family and his friends started sniffing, and then as the song built to a crescendo alongside the various comments and memories the emotion in the whole room was tangible. As the sound of the video faded, I looked around to see that my family were all holding each other, and Liam Gallagher's voice was replaced by a chorus of sobs throughout the whole room. I could barely believe it. I almost forgot that I had to take the stand and give my speech, and when I got up there the nerves returned straight away. I was so tense that the notes I had in front of me were just a jumble of words, but this was my real-life experience and I knew it all back to front having lived through it, so I would just start talking and surely the words would flow.

Around halfway through I stumbled over a sentence. My nerves coupled with the heat in the room meant I'd gone quite red, and I couldn't stop sniffing. I did panic for a moment but then I was able to carry on. People thought I was getting upset, but I was far too nervous for that. To think they were seeing me trying to hold back the tears after what they'd seen on the presentation made the audience well up even more, and by the end of my speech, I'm not sure there was a dry eye in the room. The whole thing seemed to take forever, and when I had finished there was a moment of silence. This made me feel quite awkward, but the round of applause that followed made me much more so. Even to this day, I feel very uncomfortable with compliments and credit for what I am doing, despite these being the very things that encourage me to carry on.

I was quivering with emotion, a whole mixture of relief, embarrassment, sadness, warmth, and more. So much so that I can't remember what any of Lloyd's friends said when they took the stand, although I remember that they were all fantastic, and I was so proud of them for paying tribute to their friend, my brother, in such a way. I was so grateful to them all for helping me as I imagined it would be just as nerve-wracking for them as it had been for me. They really were amazing, each and every one of them. My own enthusiasm for the campaign could only take it so far, and it was thanks to having people to share it with that I found the strength and drive to keep it going.

The evening couldn't have gone better for us really, but I was moved when Bruce asked me if he could have a copy of the presentation to play on a kind of continuous loop during the exhibition. Of course, I agreed. Bruce was someone who really boosted my determination to get the campaign going early on through his belief in what I was trying to achieve. It was his idea for me to approach schools with a view to showing the presentation to the pupils and talking to them about the campaign and the story behind it. He had encouraged Saranda to do the same. She had since become, along with her cousins, the only children to speak at a war crimes tribunal and had won the Anne Frank award. A number of schoolteachers and other staff had attended the launch event, and it had really seemed to have an impact. However, I was initially very reluctant to pursue this as I remembered how guest speakers at my school had the mickey taken out of them, and this was not something I wanted to put myself through.

I voiced my concerns to Bruce, and he reassured me that with a story like mine I was more likely to have a sympathetic response. I still wasn't completely sure I agreed with him, but something made me think it was worth a try. He had told me that he saw in me a strong belief in the need to change the world and that if I was willing to go through with the talks, I could have a massive impact.

To begin with, I worked in collaboration with Bruce, and we decided to test the waters by opening an Anne Frank exhibition at a local primary school in Wellington. I would just be reading from a sheet of paper in front of pupils and parents as part of holocaust remembrance week, and I anticipated a sympathetic reaction because of the overall theme of the event. Even still, I was shaking like a leaf as I spoke, and I felt like the sheet of paper was rustling so loud it might even drown out what I was saying. I couldn't believe I was getting so nervous in front of primary school kids. It was quite a while now since I had been one myself, but the relentless teasing was still fresh in my mind, plus speaking in front of any kind of audience made me quake with fear.

I discussed this with Bruce, and he suggested a different approach for our next talk, which would be at a local Secondary School. He said that instead of me reading from a sheet of paper I should play the presentation and then he would interview me onstage, thinking that it might ease my nerves if the focus wasn't solely on me and that he could guide the discussion to take the pressure off. I thought this was an excellent idea, and so this was what we did. I felt like if I was reading from a piece of paper that was shaking then my nerves would be more visible to the audience. This would make me feel more self-conscious and the panic would escalate. There were around 150 pupils in a theatre setup at the next event, and the new format went extremely well. Bruce spoke as well, and I clearly remember a story he told to this day, which sums up what I am hoping to achieve. In the story, there was a man walking along a beach that was littered with starfish that were stranded away from the water and were dying. He was throwing them back into the water to try and save their lives when another man who was walking along the beach stopped him.

"What are you doing?" the other man said. "There are way too many of them; you'll never save them all. Why are you even bothering? What difference will it make?"

"To the starfish I can save, it will make all the difference in the world," the first man replied, pausing momentarily before calmly returning to his task.

He then applied the story to me and what I was trying to achieve, saying that even if we cannot prevent violent attacks like the one that happened to Lloyd entirely, if we can save some families from having to experience such a horrific loss then it would make all the difference in the world to them, and so it would all have been worthwhile. This has always stuck with me and is exactly why I kept going with the campaign. I know that since Lloyd died there have been a lot of violent incidents through which someone lost their life, but if the work we've done has meant that any of these kinds of incidents have been avoided we have made a world of difference. This is what I try to never forget. Bruce said to me that I should remember I will not necessarily see if my work has made a difference because I would only hear about one of these incidents if it had a negative outcome. Therefore, just because I am not seeing evidence of my work having an impact doesn't mean I haven't potentially saved a number of lives. Maybe someone would be about to start a fight but then remember what I'd told them about Lloyd and think better of it. Maybe someone would be extra cautious when out at night after what they had heard and would avoid a violent attack that they may not have been able to otherwise.

An event at another Secondary School followed soon afterwards and, brimming with confidence from the successful event previously, I decided to write a summary to read out at the end of the presentation. I did get very nervous when reading it out, but the audience were very respectful, and I answered questions at the end. I knew nothing about the lives of any of the kids we spoke to that day but sitting among them could have been someone who was already on a violent path and could even be responsible for a death. If hearing about Lloyd's story that day made them think about the consequences of violence and to make changes over time, then just by being there and talking to them that day we would have saved their future victim's family from a whole world of pain and suffering.

Another booking came, but it seemed that disaster had struck when on the morning of the presentation Bruce called me and said that something urgent had come up, meaning he wouldn't be able to join me this time. He encouraged me to go ahead anyway, and that I would be fine without him. I wasn't sure I believed him, but the success of the previous talks had given me just enough confidence to give it a try. Looking back now I think this was all part of a plan to make me strike out on my own.

"That's probably true," laughs Bruce now. "I saw so much potential in Adam to change the world for the better. He was driven, even right at the beginning, and I was willing to give him as much time as it took to help him achieve this in any way I could, but I was also conscious of the need for him to move forward in his own way."

I have always been grateful to Bruce for his help, and it really touches me how keen he was to support me. I found out in time that he was closer to my story than I had realised.

"I became aware of what happened to Lloyd almost straight away," he recalls, "because one of the members of my church actually lived right by where the attack happened. She was quite an elderly lady, and her daughter was with her at the time. They heard a commotion outside and were later shocked to hear what had happened. Not only that, but she was due to move house soon afterwards, and it was actually the "SOLD" sign outside her house that was picked up by one of Lloyd's attackers and used to strike him."

When I think about how Bruce likened my work to Saranda's I feel humbled, and he always had ways of explaining what I was trying to achieve that were right on the money, so I knew he completely understood my aims.

"If I can use an analogy," he says. "If a young girl was to be run over and killed outside her house, the family could have one of three responses over time aside from going to the police. They might become despondent for the rest of their lives and do nothing, they might seek vengeance and try to track down the person who was driving and then murder them, or they might campaign for traffic control in the hope that other families will not suffer the same loss as them. Adam campaigned for traffic control."

I felt absolutely horrendous when the reality of giving the presentation without Bruce sank in, but I had work to do and so I didn't just collapse into a pool of terror. I adjusted my speech so I could answer the questions he usually asked but so it was just a monologue. I wasn't sure if this would work so well and thought that the interview situation actually made it a lot more engaging. My stomach was churning as I began the speech, and I felt like it was going terribly from the start. I felt like I was just bumbling my way through it, and that when it was over, I would wrap things up as quickly as I could and never come to a school again. As soon as I finished the speech the audience gave a massive round of applause. I couldn't believe it, and I was further touched when I saw some emotional responses on the faces of the pupils. This was all the encouragement I needed to carry on doing the talks on my own.

Bruce still helped me out by making the bookings at the schools and offering moral support from a distance, but I would always do the talk on my own from then on. The nerves never really went away, at least not for a number of years, but gradually I did become more confident speaking in front of an audience, and there came a time when I took over the management of the booking requests. I feel that school pupils are the most important audience for the message I am trying to put across because I believe that violence can be greatly lessened with a gradual generational change. If people learn early on about the impact violence can have, they are more likely to grow up to be non-violent. The further and wider this learning goes the more of an impact it will have on the future generations as the message is reiterated down the line.

It was another call from Bruce that perked me up on the day I had been told I would have to defer my University studies. I was feeling quite low at the time, and it was another case of perfect timing.

"Adam," he said. "You know how much I believe in the work you are doing and how proud I am of you for what you have achieved."

"Thank you," I replied, not really knowing what else to say.

"Well in recognition of this," he continued, "I want you to know that I nominated you for an Anne Frank award."

I didn't know what to say. To feel like I had messed up with my Uni studies and then to be given such high praise straight away made me feel very emotional.

"Thank you so much," I smiled. "That is so very kind of you. When will I hear the outcome?"

"Oh, no, Adam," he said. "You've actually won."

I couldn't believe it, and it literally could not have come at a better time. What's more, the ceremony would take place in London, and so I could even put a positive spin on the city where I'd experienced such disappointment not so long ago. In an even more fitting twist, the award would be presented by Cherie Blair, the wife of the Prime Minister, who I had been so disappointed not to meet! It seemed like he would be hearing about the campaign after all. At the same time, I did find it quite ironic that Cherie was presenting the award because I felt that some of her campaigns were counterproductive to mine. She was an avid human rights campaigner, and during Lloyd's trial, I could see that the idea of human rights was being distorted. The rights of Lloyd's killers were being considered at every turn whereas the rights of my family and my deceased brother were non-existent. An example of this in action was the day before the trial officially started where the defence and prosecution were making final tweaks to the case they were about to present to the jury. There was a lot of talk about "prejudicing" the trial.

Basically, we weren't allowed to look at the jury, we weren't allowed to look at the defendants, I wasn't allowed to go hell for leather at the petition because it could "prejudice" the case, meaning it could result in being thrown out. Lloyd was also not allowed anyone to stand and advocate for him besides the prosecution barrister. No friends or family were allowed to testify to his good character. The information packs that were to be given to the jury were pored over by the defence. They asked for all photographs of Lloyd, including post-mortem, to be removed because they were too emotive and "real."

All of these aforementioned things were legal, approved by the court, and completely protective of the defendants' rights and showed no regard to the rights of the victim or their voice. This just seemed so wrong. Where were Lloyd's rights in that? Where were our rights? To add insult to injury, one of the defendants was allowed a character witness, who was one of his neighbours and may have been threatened into giving him a glowing reference for all anyone knew. That was not the problem so much as the fact that he was allowed a character reference and Lloyd was not. To me, that seemed unfair and unjust. Lloyd should have been allowed exactly what the defendants were allowed. If anything, he should have been allowed more people to testify to his character as he was not able to be present himself. The overall impression was that the trial would be seen to be biased in Lloyd's favour if he was painted in too good a light or his attackers were painted in too bad a light. I wasn't interested in trying to assassinate the characters of his attackers, but I felt it was important that the jury knew the facts and had seen everything that we had. If it was any other way, then how could they come to a decision based on the true events?

During the trial, we heard that a couple of the defendants had a long history of anti-social behaviour and had been involved in plenty of violent incidents, although none quite as serious. My dad said at the time that they were ticking time bombs and it was only a matter of time before they seriously hurt or killed someone. At least one of them has since admitted this to be true. It was clear that the punishments received for their previous assaults had no impact, and they had no fear of the consequences of their actions.

I don't believe in demonising people who commit crimes, because that is similarly unlikely to lead to someone changing their ways, but there must be consequences for violent crimes especially. A few stern words will be no deterrent to someone who is capable of inflicting what happened to Lloyd and numerous others over the years. Lloyd's attackers were clearly dangerous people, and this should have been obvious to the courts, but they were still out and about and behaving in exactly the same way. This is another example of how the attitudes and values of the likes of Cherie Blair cause unintended consequences. In this instance, it is the rights of the young offender. There is so much time spent trying not to "criminalise" young people that actually no punishment or rehabilitation opportunity is even on offer. They are given very menial community sentences, where I have observed first-hand that they have no repercussions for non-attendance. It is no wonder it doesn't work, and they go through the cycle over and over. I agree that young people shouldn't have their prospects tarnished with a criminal record but if they have done something unlawful, especially if it is of a violent nature, then they need tough intervention. No "slap on the wrist," namby-pamby, wrap them up in cotton wool attitude. They must know they have done something wrong, and they must be given the support needed to make fundamental changes. Jay got this when he was sent to prison for murder. As we will find, even he wishes he had had the opportunity to get this intervention earlier on for his petty crimes, as it would have prevented the death of Lloyd and a murder conviction for him. Are we in fact damaging our young people by being too soft and too protective?

As I thought of all of these things whilst Mrs. Blair was making her speech, I felt like standing up and shouting out what I thought of her idea of "human rights." How I felt that it was part of the reason Lloyd was no longer with us and why the sentences were so minuscule. I'm glad I didn't say anything, partly because it was not the time or the place, and partly because just after she presented me with the award I spotted an army of security guards standing near her. They'd been lurking in the shadows and maybe they would have pounced!

I really enjoyed the day. My parents came with me and we had a lovely time, taking advantage of the free champagne. I must admit it went to my head a little bit, but luckily, I didn't embarrass myself in any way. I was honoured to meet some of Anne Frank's relatives and was so humbled to have been given the award. Having left London last time feeling deflated and having lost a lot of motivation to keep the campaign going, this time I left feeling inspired and determined to take this as far as I possibly could. Not everyone would agree, and there would most definitely be obstacles along the way but having someone believe in me and what I was doing who had not known me until after the campaign began was such a morale boost. It filled me with warmth.

Creating Our Key Resource

With the success of the school talks, I had grown in confidence and was wondering how I could continue the momentum I had created for the campaign. In 2008 I had the idea to take what I'd done with the presentation and turn it into a more professional video that could have a further-reaching impact. At first, I thought of including a reconstruction of the attack on Lloyd, but I thought this might be too upsetting for my family, plus I wondered if people would think I was strange for wanting to film a reconstruction of my brother's murder in the first place.

The idea for the film came about because technology was improving, and platforms such as YouTube made it possible for anyone to potentially reach a huge audience. I felt like I would be missing out on a massive opportunity by ignoring this, and a kind of prototype video I created with simple editing software seemed to have a powerful effect on audiences when I trialled it. I had the ideas and the creativity, but I felt I needed a bit of professional input and software to make the video the very best it could be. At first, I wasn't sure where to look, but then I remembered a work experience placement I had taken part in with a local film production company when I was still at school. I called them, and as luck would have it, they remembered me. They had someone in mind to hook me up with: a young filmmaker who knew Lloyd and knew the story well, so he was the perfect choice to help make my idea into a reality. I met him for an initial discussion, and it seemed like we were on the same page from the outset.

"I think you should include a reconstruction of the actual incident," he began.

"I had been thinking the same," I admitted. "But I have my reservations. I'm not sure if it would be appropriate."

"I see where you're coming from," he said, "but I think it would be very powerful. If the audience can actually see what happened, it will really reinforce the message."

I agreed, and so I mentioned our plan to my parents. Although they were not totally comfortable with the thought of a reconstruction, they didn't try to discourage me. They have never tried to stop me from doing anything I see fit that might help the campaign, and I have always been so grateful. The filmmaker agreed to help me free of charge, which I was also hugely grateful for, seeing as I was having to fund everything myself with a little help from my family at this stage. I knew there would be other costs involved, though, so I went to the local council to see if there was any funding available. They made a very generous offer of £750, which would be a massive help.

Now the ball was rolling I actually had to come up with the full concept and running order of the film. I had a vague idea, but then I hit a barrier, and nothing seemed quite right when it came to the details. I was beginning to worry, but then one night I woke up with a start, completely without explanation, and the whole idea came to me right there and then. I knew I was likely to forget everything, so I leapt out of bed and grabbed my pen and pad. Within a couple of hours of frenzied activity without a single break, I had the whole film mapped out from start to finish, and all of my concerns had vanished. It certainly felt like I had help from above.

There was still a lot to organise, and I was lucky that the filmmaker was going to take care of the camera, lighting equipment, actors, and crew. This freed me up to work on the admin side of things, and so I approached a number of local businesses in the hope that they could help me with free or reduced-cost loaning of equipment. We wanted to film on location at a local industrial estate in the dark for maximum possible authenticity. To add to the realness we were hoping to hire an ambulance, and we would need generators for an outside power source, plus a venue nearby for warmth and food. We wanted to use a cherry picker to get the best possible overhead shot, we would need to apply for a road closure and also wanted to hire some mannequins for the fight scene.

It was a lot of hard work sourcing all of those things, but it was worth it when everyone I approached offered very generous help with a little persuasion. Their kindness told me that the impact of what happened to Lloyd had been felt by the local community, and I was supported throughout. It was evidence enough that people cared about what I was trying to promote: the message of the devastating impact that violence can have. The only aspect that proved to be difficult was the road closure. I was passed from pillar to post, to begin with. I wasn't sure if it was the council, the highways agency, or the police I needed permission from, and it took months before I discovered that I had to apply to the highways agency but make sure the police and local council were notified.

There was one benefit to this final obstacle, which was that it gave me extra time to come to what would be an important decision. I had been having reservations for a while about using mannequins for the fight scene as I was worried it would look unrealistic and would lessen the impact of the message. I knew we couldn't afford professional stunt actors, but I began to wonder, after everyone was so generous with the other aspects, if anyone would be able to help. With mannequins, there would be no real possibility of close-up shots or for the realistic movement of a person, so at best it might look a little staged, and at worst it might look ridiculous.

I started Googling for companies who might be able to provide actors. The first stunt coordinator I called was absolutely lovely and after hearing just the very outline of the story she was right on board. She lived just outside London but was willing to not only travel to Somerset for two days of filming but would also gather four of her fellow stunt professionals from around the South-West and Wales to be involved and would not charge a penny for any of it. Wow! This was when I realised the potential for this campaign to go national. It was genuinely touching when local people went out of their way to help, but when someone who had no real connection to the area or to the story was willing to do so much for so little reward it just blew my mind. It told me that this was indeed a universal message that needed to travel far and wide.

The road closure fiasco was playing on my mind a little bit. I had spoken to the relevant individual in the local police force about the first night's closure and he seemed somewhat reluctant to discuss it with me but raised no objections. He seemed quite disgruntled about the whole thing really, which seemed a little odd. I called again about the second night's closure when we decided it would be needed, and I spoke to the same ray of sunshine I had before.

"This is just to let you know that we plan to have the road closed for a second night," I said after explaining who I was.

"I don't know why you keep phoning us," he muttered. "We don't need to know about this."

The whole thing seemed very odd and didn't sit well with me, especially after the disagreement I'd had with the police a few years back. I wanted to remain on good terms with all of the local organisations, and I wasn't sure why I had been dealt with in such an unfriendly way. As far as I could see I was doing everything by the book and had kept the police informed. I tried to put it out of my mind, and this was helped by the pieces of good news that kept coming. A good friend of mine and Ben's had offered to do all of the make-up for free as she was on a media make-up course at Uni. This really added something to the overall realism of the scenes.

We had originally intended to film the reconstruction where the attack had actually happened, but some of the residents had voiced concerns and so we changed our minds. There were five houses in the area we were hoping to film in, and I went door to door with Reverend Bruce Thompson to let everyone know what we had planned. Two out of the five homeowners couldn't have been more helpful, even offering the use of their water and electricity should we need it. However, one lady was clearly against the idea from the start.

After Lloyd died, people used to leave cards and flowers by a lamppost near where he was attacked, and after a while, my parents and I talked about arranging a more permanent memorial there. The council agreed to put in a small granite memorial stone with an inscription in the place of a dead tree that had been removed. We felt that it was quite hidden from view but would provide a nice tribute. The lady who lived nearby clearly disagreed and was very vocal about it. She ranted that drawing attention to Lloyd's murder happening there would devalue her house and that the memorial stone was ugly, like a tombstone. Being used to negative responses from the days of the petition, I just listened and remained polite and composed, telling her that I understood her concerns, even if that wasn't quite true. When she had closed the door Bruce looked horrified.

"I just can't understand some people," he sighed. "How could she be so unkind?"

I would have thought the same as Bruce at the beginning of the campaign but by now I had become quite thick-skinned, having seen similar responses a number of times. It was the same when the man at the next house just stared at me as I told him our plans. He clearly thought I was strange for wanting to do the film, but at least he kept his thoughts to himself, even if he made it obvious he wasn't really on board with the idea.

What really made the decision for us was when the final resident's daughter called me, I suspect having had a tip-off from one of the neighbours, and asked if we could meet to discuss the idea. I met her in a local pub, and she got straight to the point.

"I have to be honest, Adam," she said, "I'm not keen on you filming near my mother's house because she's elderly and I don't want her getting panicked thinking there's a fight happening outside."

I appreciated the fact that she'd explained this to me politely and had asked to meet me face-to-face. The last thing we wanted to do was add to anyone's stresses. It seemed that if we filmed there, we were likely to face strong opposition, which was not how we wanted the project to be, so the industrial estate it was.

In the meantime, I had returned to University to continue training as a nurse. I had been agonising over this for a while and wasn't sure if it was truly the path I wanted to take, especially after a conversation I'd had on one of my placements. There was a health visitor who seemed to be trying to convince me I would regret becoming a nurse, even though she never actually said those words. Luckily, I decided to carry on, because as soon as I started my first nursing job at the local hospital, I knew I had made the right decision. I started just before the time came to do the filming, and it felt like several areas of my life were progressing at the same time.

When the day of the filming came round, I was nervous but excited. The stunt crew arrived early to practice their scenes and I was stunned when one of them got out of the car. He was the absolute spitting image of Lloyd and could not have been more perfect to play him. The resemblance was so uncanny it was almost as if Lloyd was playing one of his pranks from beyond the grave! I couldn't stop staring at this actor, which hopefully didn't make him too uncomfortable.

The atmosphere on the first day was electric, with everything running like clockwork. The filmmaker and I were directing, and everyone did their jobs amazingly. It was one of those days when nothing went wrong, and I was feeling absolutely elated. This may seem strange given what we were filming, especially considering how much Lloyd's actor resembled him, but making this reconstruction actually helped me to gain some distance from the real events. The stunt coordinator did an amazing job with the fight scene and her professionalism was plain to see. The actors were incredible too, and I couldn't believe how realistic they made it look without anyone getting hurt. I couldn't get to sleep for quite a while that night, even though we didn't wrap up the filming until the early hours, and I couldn't wait to get going again the following evening.

I should have known by now that a high like this is almost inevitably followed by a crash, and so it proved. Early on during the second night, I saw a police car patrolling the area. It didn't really set off any alarm bells at first, but something about it seemed odd. It was a Saturday night, and they were driving around an industrial estate where they knew there would be a road closure. If they were there to make sure we were safe, then why had they not dropped by the night before? I tried to forget about it, and we put the "road closed" signs up ready to start filming. To begin with, the same buzz from the night before returned as everyone did their jobs flawlessly, but then filming was interrupted as the policemen drove straight past the "road closed" signs and we had to move all of our cables and other equipment so they could pass. As far as we could see they had no reason to be there, as I knew the road was in a horseshoe shape and so they could have gone round the other way. I was getting quite annoyed because this was wasting time and we were already scheduled for a late finish. We didn't want to be delayed any more than was necessary. I kept my cool because I knew that any amount of time spent arguing with the police was time we could have spent filming.

This happened twice more, and I was really beginning to lose my patience, but the last straw was when they came round yet again just when we had an ambulance and a crane in the road, so there was no way through. We thought they would see this and drive round the other way but instead, they drove up close and stopped in the middle of the road with their headlights on full beam. That was it! I approached the car along with a couple of the actors and the police car pulled over, but nobody got out. I went straight to the window.

"Sorry, is there a problem?" I said, trying to sound calm.

"We weren't aware of this road closure," said the officer in the driver's seat. "Please could we see your permit?"

We had brought it with us just in case, and after we showed it to them, they went on their way. The whole thing just seemed absurd. Of all the places they could have chosen to patrol on a Saturday night they came to a quiet industrial estate where we saw nobody else the whole time we were there. Their colleague had told me that they didn't need to know about it, but they said they weren't aware and wanted to see a permit. What's more, they only asked to see it when we approached them, having driven past us several times, and made us move our equipment. The whole thing seemed very fishy, and the disturbances had been annoying, but we were able to finish the rest of the filming uninterrupted. I found their actions to be arrogant, especially as they would have known we had the whole thing on camera, and to this day I'm certain they intended to disrupt our project. It was so strange.

We considered the whole experience to be a great success overall, and I was desperate to start the editing process. I knew it would be a lot less smooth; anyone who has edited a film will know that it's a lengthy process, and although we had all the footage for the reconstruction there was still a lot to gather before we could put everything together. I wanted to revisit my idea from the original presentation to include photos, comments, and newspaper headlines about Lloyd, and with the advent of YouTube, Face-book, and other social media platforms I would now be absolutely spoilt for choice rather than having just one website to choose from. Of course this meant there would be a wealth of content, but trawling through all of these places to pick out the most effective media for the video was very time-consuming. I also thought that it would have more of an impact on the viewers if we included some dialogue from different people who knew Lloyd. The filmmaker and I shared the responsibility for gathering the interview footage and you can definitely tell which ones I did. The sound quality on mine was pretty ramshackle compared to the crisp, professional audio of those that weren't!

Once we felt there was enough content, we edited the reconstruction. I was still able to distance myself from what it represented, thinking of it as a project rather than basically watching my brother's death. Once this was done, we were able to add in the other footage around it, and I wanted to include everything but we had to be quite brutal with the edit. This was a short film to be played in school assemblies rather than an hour-long documentary. It was so difficult to decide what to leave out but eventually, we got to the stage where we felt it was just the closing scene to go. Our vision for the ending was that it would explain, with a wall of familiar faces made up of other victims of random attacks, that what happened to Lloyd was not an isolated incident. It was one of many brutal attacks that had led to young lives being lost and families being devastated. It could not go on. Unfortunately, this final hurdle took a long time to overcome. No matter how hard we tried we just couldn't seem to get it right, and I think the filmmaker became quite disillusioned with the whole project by the end. It took nearly a year to complete, but when we finally did, we knew we had created a powerful film, and it had been worth taking the time over. Our local BBC reporter agreed to do a voiceover at the end, which really added something.

We were still not quite done as it happened, because for the final DVD I wanted to include some additional interviews with the local ambulance service, A&E, and the police about violence. All of these responded positively, including the police, who I was worried about approaching after what had happened during the filming. The A&E staff who had treated Lloyd didn't want to be interviewed, which I understood, but the matron of A&E gave an informative interview about the impact of violence on people and on their department.

When it came to the police, I was invited to meet with their press officer at the head office. I wasn't sure how she would respond, but I was keen to build a good relationship with the police, as I still thought we had the same goals when it came to violence reduction. I was introduced to the press officer; she seemed friendly, and keen to see the film, and she seemed very impressed by what she saw. I was offered interviews with a number of different individuals within the police force, and I was hoping that this would mean we could finally be on the same page. It quickly became clear that there was still a way to go yet.

My first interview would be with the custody sergeant at the local police station and the press officer would be there too. After she had shown her support I was actually looking forward to the meeting. She greeted me when I arrived and took me into a small office where I presumed I would be meeting the custody sergeant, but he wasn't there. Instead, there was a different officer sat at a desk. I was told he worked with schools and so was keen to see the video. I was happy with this, but as soon as he brought the film up on the computer three burly officers walked into the room and stood towering over me, blocking the doorway. I was briefly introduced to each of them, but I hadn't been told that any of them would be there and the whole meeting seemed to be the total opposite of what had been discussed. My trust was beginning to waver; in fact, I felt quite intimidated. I'm not sure if this was the intended effect, but there was a pretty awkward atmosphere.

I looked at each of the officers as the film was playing, trying to work out what they were thinking, but their expressions gave nothing away. They showed no emotion at the points in the film when I expected they might, but at least they didn't voice any objections. They waited until it had finished for that.

"You're scaremongering," said one of the officers as soon as it was over.

"The schools on my patch are never gonna touch this," said another.

I caught the eye of the officer I'd been told I was here to see originally, and he gave me what I thought was an apologetic look, but it was hard to tell. The press officer then took me off into a separate room.

"Adam," she said, "I feel I should explain that we're all concerned you have a political agenda."

"I'm not sure what you mean," I replied, "I made this film because I don't want any other families to go through what mine did, and I just want to educate people about the impact of violence. I was hoping the police would be on board with that."

I was stunned, to be honest, by what she had just told me, especially after we'd had such a positive meeting the first time. It felt like the whole setup was designed to make me lose belief in the film and to put me off the idea of showing it to anyone else. The police seemed to think the film painted them in a poor light, but from the very beginning, I had actually wanted them to be able to have more resources to tackle violent crime because I felt that they were the most effective organisation for this role. I left the station without any interviews and was quite despondent. A little later that day, though, I had a call from the officer I was originally told worked with schools.

"I'm extremely sorry about what happened today," he said, "I was just calling to check if you're okay."

"Thank you," I said, "I am okay, although that really didn't go the way

I was expecting to be honest."

"I bet," he sighed. "I'd still like to meet with you if that's okay?"

"Okay, but I'm not meeting at the station."

We met at a coffee shop and I was on my guard when I first arrived, but I left the meeting feeling much better about the whole experience. It seemed that not everyone in the police force was against my campaign. This officer apologised again for his colleagues' behaviour and said that he worked in schools and would be keen to show the film in a few of them with me there to answer questions. We built up a good working relationship over time, and he always seemed genuine in his support of the film, even though I remained wary for quite a while. I wondered if he was just the "good cop" keeping an eye on me and reporting back to his colleagues.

I hoped there might be an opportunity still to include an interview with the police in the DVD, and at first, it seemed like it might happen. The press officer contacted me and said that I could interview a couple of officers. However, there were conditions. I would have to include one of the interviews in the main film, put an age restriction on it, and make the website that would host the film password protected.

I did consider this for a while, but I had already shown the film to a child psychologist who had deemed it suitable for year 9 and above. We hadn't planned on age restricting the film and felt it should be left to the discretion of the teacher whether their class should see it. I decided to offer the police a compromise: I would include an interview with one of the officers in the main film but I would not be restricting access to it in the way they requested. This didn't go down well, and they weren't willing to grant any interviews unless I met all of their requests. I said that this was a shame, but I wasn't willing to potentially stop a huge number of my target audience from seeing the film to fit in with their wishes. No compromise was reached. To even include a police interview in the main film would have meant extra editing time close to the launch, and would have been stressful, but I would have been willing to do it. Throughout the whole campaign, I tried to listen to my gut feeling and was not willing to compromise on anything that felt wrong.

The launch had been scheduled for the anniversary of Lloyd's death and took place at a local arts centre. A lot of people were invited from local authorities, schools, potential funders, youth offending teams, and the police. Most of them came, and I made a speech after the film had been shown. It should have been an encouraging evening, and most who attended were very impressed, giving some wonderful feedback. Alarm bells were ringing already, though, when I spotted two of the policemen who had criticised the film at the station in the audience. Sure enough, as soon as I had finished my speech, in which I included statistics from NHS Emergency Departments to help explain how significant an issue violence was, they piped up.

"You can't trust those statistics," one of them called out. "The only ones you should be going by are ours and those from the Home Office."

I was no expert at the time, but I had done enough research to know that the police's statistics don't paint the whole picture because they only include crimes that are reported and, moreover, they only include crimes that are prosecuted or charged. Those that were dropped were also dropped from the stats. Not all violent crimes are reported, for a number of reasons. People are afraid of recriminations if they get a violent person in trouble with the police, or they might think that nothing will be done, or that the incident was not too serious. Whether the officers knew this or not they seemed very keen to belittle the message behind the film, and it did take the gloss off the uniform praise I received from most who attended. At the end of the evening, a senior officer who had come along with them told me that the film was excellent and that he was sure it would have a powerful impact. As he praised my efforts his two colleagues silently fumed nearby.

Getting the video onto a website ended up being quite an ordeal. Again, web design didn't have the all-inclusive, straightforward possibilities it does today and so I didn't really look into doing it myself. One local company offered to set a website up free of charge, and I was delighted, but the day of the launch got closer and closer and it didn't look like the work was going to be completed on time. Another time I could have held fire, but I wanted the launch to go ahead as scheduled and the film being available to watch on the website was a vital element, so I had no option in the end but to look for another company to get it done at short notice. I was extremely fortunate to have a contact who was able to help, again free of charge, but then the first company didn't take kindly to this at all and demanded that I paid them for their time. After quite a heated exchange I agreed to pay them a small amount and had to do so out of my own pocket, but the website was up and running in time for the launch and so ultimately all was well.

One of the main positives of the launch event had been that the local head of the Youth Offending Team had been very impressed with the film and had ordered twenty copies of the DVD for each of their offices in Somerset. This was absolutely fantastic, and initial feedback suggested that it was an extremely valuable resource for young offenders, which was one of the biggest aims of the whole project. Over time, though, a different picture emerged and we heard that the Youth Offending Team had stopped using the film. I was keen to find out why, as there seemed to have been a sudden U-turn, and after a discussion with a local magistrate who supported the campaign, we set up a meeting with someone from the YOT. We came away more perplexed than we already were because the officer we met with couldn't answer many of our questions and seemed to be completely in the dark as to why this would have happened.

Eventually, we found out that the manager of the Youth Offending Team was a good friend of the local police superintendent, whose husband was a teacher at a local public school and had deemed the film to be too violent for his pupils. It seemed that they'd all talked and the teacher's view had rubbed off on the Youth Offending Team's manager, so they decided it was too violent for young offenders and might be counterproductive. They thought it might inspire them to be violent rather than making them think twice. DVD sales had been increasing, so this was a huge disappointment, especially as young offenders were one of the key groups I was looking to target with the film. It felt like a huge setback, but despite my ongoing battle to get the police onside, I knew the campaign was going from strength to strength on the whole, and we were creating a real legacy for Lloyd, of which he would be proud. I was far from done yet.

Growing the Impact

After the success of the film, some of my friends suggested it might be a good idea to stop the campaign and move on with my life. I understood what they were saying, but I disagreed. In fact, I saw the film as just the beginning. The original website we made was called Stand Against Violence, and it featured a map where the locations of violent incidents around the local town could be pinned. It ended up being closed down because it was unsustainable for us at the time, but the name and the logo we used would soon be returning.

Firstly, I thought there was a lot more we could do in schools with the film. I approached a Personal, Social, Health, and Economic Education (PSHE) teacher from a school I'd already been to, asking her to help me develop a lesson plan and some workshops to be delivered in schools so that there could be a more structured interaction with the pupils. She agreed, even though she was worried about potential redundancy at the time, and once again offered her time for free. When I think back to how many people did this I am almost speechless. She was a natural at working with young people and helped me to prepare an engaging and highly emotive workshop that would end up being delivered in schools all over the region, not just in Somerset. I started doing talks in some of the neighbouring counties, the furthest afield being at a school in Plymouth.

I decided it was time to get a bit more serious with the whole campaign. What happened at the launch event for the film with the police officers trying to belittle me made me realise I needed to get properly clued up on the topic of violence prevention, so if anyone tried to make me sound clueless they would be in for a surprise! The best way to make sure I did this, in my mind, was to turn the campaign into an official charity. I had no idea how to do such a thing, but as with most things the information is out there if you're willing to look for it. The chance to create a lasting legacy for Lloyd was all the motivation I needed, so I started doing my homework.

The first stumbling block was that you needed £5,000 in the bank in order to register a charity. I didn't have £5,000 and so I contacted the charity commission to ask why a not-for-profit charity would be expected to have that much money to begin with. Nobody seemed to understand why I would ask this question, and it felt like most people just accepted it, but one man I spoke to was very kind and helpful. He told me that the £5,000 could be a pledge. I asked my parents if they would be willing to do this, and they agreed straight away. Once more I was overwhelmed with the belief they showed in me, and the unending support for what I wanted to achieve.

I also needed a board of trustees and managed to put one together from people I had met through the campaign, alongside a few people who were recommended by those I had already asked. This was tricky to begin with, as obviously the charity was deeply personal to me, and so it seemed like the trustees were afraid of upsetting me by disagreeing with anything I said. I explained to them that it was vital for the charity to be able to move forward and that they had to speak up if they disagreed with me on anything. Over time they began to question any decisions of mine they were unsure about, and even if it might have upset me a little bit under the surface it was one of the main reasons I made the campaign into a charity. I needed to be challenged and to know I was making the right decisions having discussed them properly with people who might offer a different perspective. It really helped us to progress.

I also had to write a charitable objective. The original one, which was very much tailored towards violence prevention, was rejected by the charity commission, but then the helpful man I'd spoken to before rewrote it for me and just made it very simple. We were ready to go.

I had an opportunity to get involved in a TV show called ITV Fixers, which supported campaigns run by young people that helped other young people. After applying I had a very successful initial meeting. I pitched the idea of a book, but they were looking for something more instant and were hoping for a film of some kind. The film we had already made was too long, and so we came to a mutual decision that we would create an advert. It made sense to me that a whole book, and the message that went with it, could not be easily summarised for a TV show. Also, it wasn't very visual, so I was happy with the advert idea. I actually had very little to do this time in terms of the organisation, which was very welcome. I was still very much involved with the ideas, and they kept me in the loop during the whole process, but basically, all the logistics were taken care of. This removed a lot of the stress.

The concept was for an imagined scenario on a night out when everyone would be shown to be having a good time, but then more and more alcohol would be consumed and on the way home one of the main characters would get in a fight. He would end up being badly injured. We would see the man who assaulted him getting arrested the next morning, and so we would see the impact on his life also, but the final scene would show the man he attacked being spoon-fed mashed up food by his mum, unable to do anything for himself. When I watched it back I found the final scene to be haunting, especially when the man's head lolled to one side as the spoon was being put to his mouth, showing that he was badly brain damaged and could not survive without constant care. The whole thing was slightly longer than I would have liked. The lady I worked with on the editing was clearly very good at what she did, but we just didn't click in the same way I had with the previous filmmaker, and so I ended up taking it away and editing most of it myself before passing it back to her to add the finishing touches.

I was very happy overall with the finished product, and I felt it would make an excellent addition to our workshops. The final scene, depicting the brain-injured man, did stay with me for a while and made me think about how it could have happened to Lloyd instead of him dying. I felt guilty for thinking so, but I would rather he had died than lived the rest of his life with such severe brain damage. I know it was an opinion my family shared, and I think Lloyd would even agree. He had been so active and full of life that to be unable to think or do anything for himself would have been no kind of life at all. If he had been in a wheelchair but able to think and communicate he would have found plenty of ways to remain active, and no doubt plenty of ways to be cheeky, but if he was there in body and not in mind? Would that be any kind of life for anyone? It takes a truly horrific situation for that to be the silver lining, but I really did believe it was better for him to have died than to have continued to exist without really living. The message of the advert was that one single act of violence can ruin your life and the lives of others forever, and I knew it put this across powerfully.

When the advert was done I was invited once again to the capital for a celebratory event at the ITV London studios, along with several other people from projects that had been featured on the show. It would be broadcast live on ITV's online channel and I would be interviewed about Stand Against Violence as part of it, so I jumped at the chance. I went along with Ben and a friend. This country mouse still wasn't used to the frantic pace and vastness of the capital, and I was still a little freaked out by the tube system, but we found the studios and I began to enjoy myself once we had settled in. It felt like a big deal, and I began to mingle with the other guests, trying to make the most of the occasion.

After a while, I met a girl I'd chatted to a little bit online. She ran a branch of the "STOP!" campaign, an organisation that had been set up by a guy I briefly knew who had lost a loved one to knife crime. Like me, he just wanted to try and stop the same thing happening to other families. The girl I met was a single mother to a very young daughter, who she told me had come from a violent relationship, and she'd lost two of her family members to knife crime. She seemed very dedicated to the cause and I thought she was amazing for taking on so much after all she had been through. I even nominated her for an Anne Frank award.

She seemed very friendly at first, and we were getting on well, but as soon as she found out I was going to be interviewed her whole energy changed and she started asking me to mention the "STOP!" campaign. If she'd asked once I would have thought nothing of it, but she got quite relentless about it, as if she was trying to bully me into talking about her cause. I put it down to her dedication, but I did find the whole thing a little intense and it made me feel more cautious around her.

When my time came to be interviewed I realised I would only have a few minutes. This was a chance to get significant national exposure for Stand Against Violence, and I wasn't as nervous as I might have been because I couldn't see any of the large audience who might be watching. All the same, to know it would be going out live did add some pressure. In such a short space of time I had to keep on topic, and to suddenly name drop another organisation would have seemed out of place. I was pleased with this golden opportunity to promote our cause, but my new friend made no secret of the fact that she was put out when I didn't mention hers. I have to admit this made me feel a little uncomfortable; we'd only just met.

On my return to Somerset, I was thinking about how best to take Stand Against Violence forward. We were an official charity now but were still only just beginning and so none of us really knew what we were doing to begin with. A few board members came and went early on as we were finding our feet, but there was a core group, including myself of course, who had been there from the start. I was conscious of the fact that, as with any charity, the trustees would have to be voted in at each Annual General Meeting (AGM), and so in theory I could lose my place on the board. Obviously, this was unthinkable for me, as I'd put so much into this enterprise over several years now. With this in mind, I ensured that there was a clause in the charity's constitution stating that founding board members could not be voted out and would remain in their roles unless they stood down.

To begin with, we just bumbled along and took any opportunities that came up without actively seeking them, but as time went on and we agreed that we were in this for the long haul I realised that we would have to develop a strategy and that I would have to become more business-minded. I knew of an organisation that helped other charities to develop business skills. They asked us to come in for a meeting, and it was clear that they had some reservations.

"I hope it doesn't seem insensitive for us to say this," they began, "but we have often seen charities that are set up after the loss of a loved one lose their drive after a few years. The charity is set up as a kind of coping mechanism, and then as time moves on it has served its purpose, and those who started it find themselves wanting to move on."

"I understand," I smiled, recalling that people had suggested this very thing not long ago. "But this has been going as a campaign for five years now, and the reason we're coming to you is because we feel we're only just getting started. We want a long-term strategy so we know we'll keep progressing."

They were reassured by this, and they helped us to develop a business plan, giving us lots of useful advice as well. Following this, we had a very productive board meeting, where we brainstormed ideas on a flip chart and came to some important decisions. Perhaps the key one was for us to separate into a youth branch and a main branch. This came about after we had recently manned a stall at a family fun day where our face painting table was surrounded by very young children and was right next to a huge banner that told the story of Lloyd's murder. This made for a very uncomfortable few hours, and we were still keen to engage with young children but realised that we would have to do so in the right way, with a proper strategy in place. We planned to have a specific website for younger people and to engage with them in different ways to the workshops we had developed for older children. The main branch would deal with the continuation of these workshops and the expansion of them into new locations, as well as fundraising and continuing to build a reputation for the charity. With a lot of hard work, we had a business plan in place that we really believed would enable us to deliver on all of our aims.

The charity continued to gain recognition, and I felt like we'd truly arrived when we won the Mayor's Choice Award in 2010, followed by the Citizenship Award from the local council in 2011. There was one particular councillor who was very supportive of Stand Against Violence and she invited me along, several months after the award, to a meeting where a vote would be taking place. I was told that they would be voting on whether to support the charity as a council, and I felt that if they did it would be validation for all of our hard work over the previous six years. I was feeling quite nervous in this room full of local influential figures, even though one couple were acquaintances of mine. The moment arrived.

"All in favour?" said the mayor, and every hand in the room went up without hesitation. I tried to stop my mouth from falling open.

"So that confirms a unanimous decision to support Stand Against Violence," he continued.

I was absolutely speechless. The local council seemed to think that our charity was one the town could be proud of and that they should give their full backing to. A couple of the councillors came to speak to me outside as I was leaving and said congratulations. I became totally overwhelmed and couldn't hold back the tears. It was just like you see on TV when someone cries after winning an award, when you have worked so hard and believe in something so much, it's just so heart-warming when you receive recognition for it all. Once I regained my composure I felt elated and was told that I should contact them and they would see that there was regular support in place.

The immediate future of the charity seemed to be secure, especially as there was a cash prize that went along with the award, but before too long the bubble was burst. I found out that the support was time-limited, and a year later when I was trying to secure funding I contacted the council but was told that their support had only been for a year and that they could no longer help me. I was gutted and felt quite embarrassed that I'd got so emotional in front of them. What had seemed like the start of such an exciting time was basically just a hollow promise.

This was especially disappointing because one of the more mundane aspects of running a charity is having to secure funding, and although it's not as exciting as seeing young people inspired by your work it is vital in order to keep your endeavours going. I thought this aspect was going to be taken care of for a while, but instead we were quickly back to square one. Writing funding applications is time-consuming and can often be hours and hours of work for no reward. It always feels like the time could have been much better spent, but when a bid is successful it's a great feeling. Ironically, it becomes harder to obtain funding the more established a charity becomes. A lot of the big funders, such as the National Lottery, often favour new projects. It's great that the funding is there to get new charitable ventures off the ground, but what about the organisations with a proven track record who need to continue existing work? It can take up a lot of valuable time trying to source the funds.

At this time I felt we needed to be ambitious if we were going to survive as a charity in the long run. I'd heard of an event in Birmingham called The Education Show. I thought that to attend would be a fantastic opportunity for us and that it might help us to really establish our workshops on a bigger scale as well as meeting some potential funders. There is often a cost involved in having a stand at these events, but at the local ones it's usually quite a modest amount. For The Education Show, it seemed we would have to stump up a few thousand pounds. This did feel like quite a risk, but I thought it represented a chance to make Stand Against Violence a national charity. I applied to the National Lottery for some funding to attend and they gave us £7,000! I was very pleased, and my dad helped me to hand-make a stand, so I thought it would actually end up being no financial risk at all. How wrong I was.

Once again I realised how naïve I'd been, as the booking process for the show revealed a number of hidden costs and I was stunned to learn that just having a stand there would be nearly £10,000. What's more, that was the charity rate! I dread to think what somebody would have to pay to attend as a business. Could any potential benefit be worth such a huge upfront cost?

I really hoped that it would be worth it, and before we went I felt optimistic that it would be the best decision we'd ever made. A few of us travelled up to Birmingham for the three days of the event, and it became clear pretty quickly that we were going to be disappointed. Most who attended were from Primary Schools, and at that time our youth branch was way behind our main branch. Really we had nothing for primary school children at the time. We tried to remain upbeat and told each other that things would probably pick up as the event went on, but by the end of it I felt disgusted when I thought of the amount of money we'd wasted. At least my conscience was clear because the money had come from a funding organisation and not from peoples' donations, but it still felt like something we shouldn't be doing as a charity.

Nothing had really been gained from the experience apart from the knowledge that we would have to be more careful in the future. They do say "you have to speculate to accumulate" but when you're a charity, to spend that amount of money on something that ended up being futile just isn't on. I was perplexed as well as to how the National Lottery wouldn't fund any ongoing running costs or salaries but had been prepared to invest this. I had been so sure that this was our chance to really boost our profile and cement our credibility, but it was time to think again.

Thinking Big

The Education Show flop was massively disappointing, but I was determined for us to catch our break. The need to think big was something we'd discussed at length in our meetings, and so when I heard of a programme run by O2 called Think Big it felt like a sign. The programme was designed to help people under the age of 25 with training and funds to set up and run projects. I still fit into that category, just, at the time and so I applied as an individual. Looking back now, this was the moment when Stand Against Violence started to become what it is today.

As with the stunt coordinator who was so helpful with the video and the guy at the charity commission who assisted us so much, I spoke to a lady at O2 who seemed to take to my story straight away and could not have been more supportive of our work. She put me up to receive the award without a second thought. What this meant initially was a trip to Cardiff for a day's training in business development along with £500 for the charity. This was not a huge sum but we were able to use it to help gain support from some local authorities, and this helped lend some credibility to our work.

The training day in Cardiff was a really useful experience. It was more of a refresher of ideas I was familiar with from my college days but the key difference was that I now had a real working context to apply it all to, and I was able to go back to the board with a renewed focus. It seemed I had made quite a splash with the top dogs at O2 as well. I think it helped that

I was one of the first people on the programme, and so their enthusiasm for it was still very high. This, coupled with my emotional story, meant that they really took notice of me and I really believe this helped me to advance through the programme onto bigger and better opportunities.

There were different levels of the programme, and my application for level 2 was successful, but I had a dreadful sinking feeling when I learnt that this involved a residential course. The last residential I had been on was in Secondary School and I hated every moment. I was not one of the "cool kids," and I detested all of the silly games and activities, just hoping I would get through them all without giving the other kids ammunition to tease me. I was still quite young and so I imagined this one would be much the same. I phoned the organiser before going and explained, in no uncertain terms, that I would not be getting myself muddy or getting involved in any zany activities. As far as I saw it I was there to learn, and not for any kind of socialising. She tried to reassure me, probably realising that I was just nervous.

I ended up really enjoying the experience. As soon as I got there I got chatting to some great people who were running fantastic projects, and I would keep running into them at future O2 events. We became almost like the O2 community. I even got into the spirit of things with some "energiser" games and really let my guard down. There were classes as well, and some of the top guys from O2 were on hand to give us valuable advice. I found the top marketing guy's talk on promotions particularly game-changing. To hear from people with a proven track record who were at the very top of their fields inspired me, and I returned home really feeling like I had the tools to push Stand Against Violence onto bigger and further-reaching opportunities.

As part of level 2 we also received a larger amount of funding, through which we were able to put my newfound skills and knowledge to use in delivering a couple of all-day workshops for local schools. The O2 funding covered all costs, and there would be a presentation of Lloyd's story followed by self-defence, first aid, and violence prevention workshops. I thought the kids would love the idea of taking part as it would be a break from their normal routine, but the whole day would really make them think, and they would learn valuable new skills. Sadly, some of the schools seemed to think that because the day was free to attend it would not be worth their time. One of them even neglected to let me know this after they had originally booked on, so I only found out they weren't joining us when I called them on the morning to see if they'd been delayed. Those who did attend were full of praise and said they would be booking us to come in, but none of them actually did. Perhaps their opinion changed when they considered the fact they'd actually have to spend money. I wasn't too disheartened, because I knew we'd developed an excellent package that would really inspire teenagers and make many see violence in a new way, knowing what the consequences can be.

I knew the skills and ideas I was learning were helping us to be more professional as an organisation and to deliver our message more effectively. It was sometimes hard to get schools to agree to bookings; letters were ignored, I was sent around the houses when I phoned and sometimes the offers of free workshops just weren't taken. It was an area I thought we should persist in despite the setbacks, and I was proven right over time.

Being on the O2 programme began to mean there were more opportunities than it was possible for me to attend. I was working full-time in nursing, and so I had to watch a number of excellent opportunities go by. It was like they were floating past me on a fast-flowing river and I couldn't find a long enough stick to reach them and bring them over to the bank. We had no regular money as a charity and so we were unable to fund even a part-time role for me, which would have enabled me to take full advantage of the programme. There were networking events, conferences, and even chances to travel abroad and meet some of the movers and shakers of O2 Europe. It would all have become quite maddening but then an opportunity came up that was just the kind of thing we'd been looking for, although there was no guarantee that we would be successful. Basically, O2 were thinking of extending the reach of the Think Big programme and so would be showing adverts in cinemas nationwide to showcase some of the projects.

One project would be chosen from each region: north, south, east, and west. We were extremely keen to be chosen and so we put a lot of effort into our application. When I got the news that we'd been successful I was absolutely buzzing. So many people loved going to the cinema, and so we would be reaching a huge audience. What's more, O2 pretty much took on the responsibility for making the advert, but with our input of course. It was shown in cinemas all over our region, but that was just the beginning. As part of the package, we also had media training and even had a celebrity supporter assigned to us.

I'd not heard of Wretch 32, and neither had any of my country bumpkin friends, but a little research told me that he was creating quite a buzz in London, so I felt that we would be reaching a new audience with his support. We were originally going to be assigned Plan B, who everyone knew about, but there was some concern that he would seem like an odd choice because it could be argued that some of his work glorified violence. Instead, we hooked up with Wretch. He talked about us, and his reasons for supporting us, in a number of interviews with national publications, and I'm sure his support was genuine. He spoke of how, as a young teenager in Tottenham, he'd seen older guys with expensive watches and flashy cars and wanted to follow in their footsteps. He learnt that they were "bad boys" and so this was what he wanted to be, but then he found another way to succeed through music. He became quite appalled by the culture of violence, especially when he saw several friends get caught up in it. I was given an opportunity to meet him, and it seems like we could have had a fascinating and very productive discussion, but the first time we met was quite a strange experience.

Wretch 32 and his PR officer met with me in London. As with the petition early on I might have been a little naïve, but I imagined him listening intently to my story before discussing ways in which we could collaborate. Instead, Wretch was on his phone for every minute of the conversation working on a new track while he spoke to me. Meanwhile, his PR lady watched him like a hawk, trying to make sure he said and did the "right" things. Seeming like I had his undivided attention would have been a start.

I could be wrong, but my impression was that they thought I should be grateful for being lent some of his precious time. I would later learn that this is often the way when something is arranged through a celebrity's management or PR team. Meeting me was viewed as one of a number of engagements that day. We tried to chat, but let's just say it didn't seem like we hit it off especially, and I found the whole thing pretty awkward. When Tottenham and Taunton collide.

A more positive experience was when I was invited to a launch event for the advert at a private cinema. I got to spend some time with people from other projects who had become friends of mine through the programme, and I accidentally ran up quite a bill on 02's tab with one of the guys! I was very impressed with all of the others as individuals, and they had some fantastic projects, so this was a special night. It felt like a celebration of what had started with a speculative application but ended up being an incredible opportunity both for me and for Stand Against Violence. It had a huge impact on raising the charity's profile and made me more confident as a person.

There was also a local launch event, where we got to choose a film to be played after the advert. There were several to choose from, and we felt the one that would most fit with our message was "Tinker, Tailor, Soldier, Spy." It may not have glorified violence and was certainly appropriate for our audience, but let's just say it wasn't the most exhilarating film, and as it went on we felt more and more awkward. The feeling that everyone would be judging us for choosing this film got more intense, and time seemed to almost stand still. The poor mayor was clearly struggling to stay awake, and so would we have been if we hadn't been feeling so terribly embarrassed about the whole thing. Oops!

We saw the funny side, and soon afterwards I was really excited to hear that 02 were looking to build on the success of the launch event by organising the Think Big Gig at the Indigo 02 in London. Young people from all over the capital would be coming along to have a good time, to see some exciting live performances and to hear about the projects, including ours. This was massive and was especially meaningful for me as it was the kind of thing Lloyd would have loved. Wretch 32 and Chipmunk would be performing, and both were popular rap artists at the time, so the crowd would be excited to see them. I've never been much of a rap fan myself; I'm a cheesy pop guy! I didn't mind, though, because I knew I would have an opportunity to deliver our message to a huge crowd that was made up of exactly the kind of people we were hoping to reach.

I'd been terrified back in the early days at the thought of addressing a small room of primary school children, so speaking to several thousand hyped-up young adults would be a real test of how far I'd come. One of the trustees, who had been a friend of Lloyd's, said she would come with me for moral support. I knew I would be talking for a while before introducing Wretch 32, who they had all come to see. He would say a few words with me still onstage and then I would step aside for him to perform. I expected they would see any "friend of Wretch" as a friend of theirs, and so I would have their attention. If he spoke about the cause when he was standing next to me it would reinforce the message of my speech and would be more memorable to them. I wasn't naïve enough to think it was me they would be there to see, but I thought this was where Wretch's support would help me to get our message far and wide. I was nervous but excited.

I was so grateful to my fellow trustee for coming with me. She was a wonderful help, and we joked that she was my "wingman." By the time I had to make my speech the atmosphere was absolutely burning, and there was a real sense of anticipation. The evening had pressed on and the lights were on inside the venue, so I couldn't see the crowd. I was tingling with adrenaline, and there were pins and needles running up my spine and all the way down my arms to my fingertips. I asked my wingman if she would hold my jacket because I was overheating and perspiring. She took it without a word and smiled, telling me "Don't worry, you've got this."

It was time. I took a deep breath and stepped out on stage to a roar from the crowd. It wouldn't take Sherlock Holmes to work out that I wasn't Wretch 32, but they knew the moment was near. I had written down a brief speech, thinking that if I tried to freestyle I was likely to stumble over my words, and even though the paper might be quivering in my hand at least I would know what to say, and the crowd may not be close enough to notice. I read out the speech with no issues and the audience were respectful throughout, so I was relieved to be able to introduce the man they were all waiting to see.

"Thank you all for listening," I said, amid a huge round of applause as I tried not to burst into tears. "Now please welcome onstage . . . Wretch 32!"

The audience went absolutely berserk, and I looked over to the side of the stage, but instead of the man himself smiling and bounding towards me, microphone in hand, I saw a guy I didn't recognise frantically waving his arms. I glanced at the audience before walking over to see what was happening.

"Wretch has changed his mind, mate!" he said. "He's going onstage with Chipmunk later on."

"Erm . . ."

What?! I looked back at the crowd and instead of seeing thousands of excited young people, I saw a bunch of roaring lions in my mind's eye. I'd just told them that their favourite rapper was about to come on stage without realising it was a lie! What could I possibly tell them now?

"You gotta let them know, man!" said the messenger, his wide eyes and clenched teeth adding the unspoken word: "Now!"

Well, at least it wasn't quite the worst thing that had ever happened to me. I'd just spoken about that moments before. Somehow I found the courage to go back on stage and break the news. I can't remember what I said, but I basically apologised and improvised a little bit before dashing for the sanctuary of the backstage bar area. After I'd had a little cry in a toilet cubicle I got myself together. My euphoria had been replaced by total humiliation in the click of a finger. I tried to put it all to one side because I had to go back to my wingman and tell her how much I appreciated her being there. I made sure my eyes were dry and that I seemed composed before I headed back out to find her. Poor girl was still holding my jacket, so I took it straight away.

"Who does Chipmunk think he is?" she said, looking exasperated.

"Wretch," I corrected her. "I'm sure he had his reasons."

"No, I mean Chipmunk," she insisted. "When you were on stage, I asked this guy to hold your jacket so I could take a pic. He just looked me up and down and went 'Nah, mate!'"

"No way," I said. "What an asshole."

"I know," she said. "I told him he was rude, and he just smirked and walked off. Then some guy came up and said, 'You do know that was Chipmunk, right?'"

I gasped, but I couldn't help laughing.

"I don't care who he is," she continued. "Manners cost nothing."

We both burst into fits of laughter and I gave her a hug.

"Well said," I smiled. "Come on, let's go and get a drink!"

My humiliation was almost forgotten as the drinks flowed and I caught up with my drinking partner from the launch event, who joined us for a while. I always enjoyed catching up with him at the O2 events, and the three of us were having a great time. He left after a while because it was his turn onstage.

"Another drink?" I asked my wingman.

"Yeah, but I'll get these," she said. "I'm just going to the loo a minute, but there's some money in my purse. You can pay with that."

I went to get the drinks, and when I was putting the change in her purse I was stunned to notice that she carried the same picture of Lloyd that I always had in my wallet. I was so moved by this. It was almost like Lloyd was with us. The night may not have gone exactly as I was hoping it would, but I knew that Lloyd would be so proud of all I had achieved so far, and this outweighed any lingering embarrassment from the onstage fiasco. As I thought about it all I was able to reason that our aim was to stop one family from having to go through what we did, and maybe my speech tonight would end up doing that in some way. Thousands of people had heard it, so hopefully at least some of them would take something away from it. As soon as I'd seen the photo I was reminded of what this was all for, and although events rarely go perfectly, this one had given us a chance to reach a lot of people who may otherwise not have heard our message. Job done.

It was also as a result of this gig that the girl I'd met from the "STOP!" campaign came back into the picture. I hadn't realised that she was involved with O2 and had a hand in organising this event. An alarm bell rang at the ITV Fixers event where I first met her in person and since then I'd become more wary.

She would regularly call me, and it often left me feeling uncomfortable. She either spent ages telling me about deeply personal issues, not really knowing me too well, or called for a chat, but I could hear her typing on the other end of the line as I spoke. I began to feel like she was a little bit false, and the night of the gig confirmed my suspicions. It all started when she said in the bar that Chipmunk was her cousin. There was no reason to doubt this on face value, but later on when we were all heading back to the hotel in a taxi, she mentioned that she'd lost six members of her family to knife crime when she had told me before it was two. She had spoken at the Labour Party Conference, which had been set up through O2, and said to a large audience that it was eight members of her family she'd lost. I don't know how she thought she would get away with lying about it, especially as there were BBC cameras following her to events for an upcoming documentary.

A camerawoman had been following her at the Think Big Gig and wasn't treated with a lot of respect. At one point during a conversation with me, the girl got up and shouted "Follow!" at the camerawoman. I didn't know where to look. A number of us had a drink at the hotel bar without her present, and it seemed we all had our suspicions. I felt awful for doubting that she'd been through such trauma, and I felt sorry for her if she was making it up because I knew she must have some serious issues to live her life on a lie in that way, but the way she treated people was not right.

When the documentary was broadcast everything came out and I discovered that there were more untruths than I'd even realised. It started off showing her in a good light and we saw her receiving a standing ovation for her speech at the Labour Party Conference. After this, though, the reporter's whole tone changed on the voiceover as she explained how they began to suspect the girl wasn't genuine. Again I began to feel sorry for her, having her lies exposed on national TV so everyone would judge her. The reporter had found out that the people she'd said she had lost to knife crime were actually Facebook friends of hers who she still had regular contact with. They even tried to call her on camera, but as soon as they questioned her she hung up. I found out that she didn't even have a daughter, and I felt quite embarrassed to have nominated her for an award. All the same, I held no grudge against the girl, and I hope this whole experience inspired her to change. She clearly craved attention for reasons we may never understand, and attention was definitely what she got. I wish her well, and I do genuinely hope she's okay. The show ended up doing Stand Against Violence no harm either because I was interviewed as someone from a similar project and a lot more people heard what I had to say.

Discord on the Board

The opportunities with O2 just kept on coming, and the contrast with The Education Show was astonishing. I'd been so convinced that the event in Birmingham was the way to catapult Stand Against Violence towards national recognition and outreach, but we spent the best part of £10,000 and had nothing to show for it. Getting on the O2 programme had cost basically nothing but it had set in motion a string of events that took us further than I could have imagined when I first heard the application had been successful. The problem remained, however, of my full-time job elsewhere making it impossible to take full advantage of all that O2 could offer us. I watched my friends and peers from the O2 programme land presenting roles, jet all over the place, and gain levels of exposure for their campaigns that I thought we needed a slice of.

"That could be us," I said to our board, having told them about the opportunities that were passing us by. "But not with our current setup. What I'm proposing is that we apply for some funding for me to become a part-time paid CEO of Stand Against Violence, enabling me to reduce my hours working as a nurse. That way we can maximise the potential of this programme that has already given us so much."

The more opportunities that went begging the more the answer became clear. If I was able to divide my working hours between the hospital and the charity, rather than just pursuing the aims of the charity in my spare time, we could reach a level that would be impossible to get to with things the way they were. I thought the board would be in total agreement, and I think at one time they would have been, but I realised how swayed they had been by a new trustee. She'd joined the board a while back, and at first I thought she was lovely, and just what we needed. I'd always been trying to increase the professionalism of the charity, and this lady helped us to put proper charity governance and policies in place, which I knew little about, as well as really helping to develop our volunteering branch. Unfortunately, her effect on the other trustees was almost bewitching. Whereas up until now they had been excited to move the charity forward and went with their hearts, I felt like they were suddenly adopting a zero risk, red tape, bureaucratic approach, and we really suffered because of it.

Suddenly everything needed a policy, and decisions that would have taken a week took many months. Not every trustee was on board with the new way of thinking but the majority were, and so I couldn't overrule them with a casting vote on any decisions that I was convinced weren't the right ones. There were quite a few of these as well. I was starting to think I might have created a rod for my own back by turning the campaign into a charity in the first place. I thought that doing so would give us credibility, increased professionalism, and unlimited potential for growth. For quite a while this was exactly what it did, but there had now come a time when we were focusing way too much on the professional side of things and forgetting why we'd started the charity in the first place. At least that was my opinion.

A clique seemed to be developing within the board, led by the newest member, and they told me that they weren't sure if I could remain on the board if I became a paid employee. I did see their point on this, as it could be a conflict of interests, so I asked one of the trustees to find out what the charity commission's take on it would be. I was told that this wouldn't be a problem in theory, but the board would have to decide whether it would be allowed. They said they would form a sub-group to put together a job description, then I could add anything I felt was missing, after which they would decide if I should be given the role. I must admit the whole thing felt very strange to me. I never wanted Stand Against Violence to be a dictatorship and was keen for the other trustees to have their say, but over this matter, I felt they were being needlessly bureaucratic. It was a huge waste of time.

The whole process took five months, during which they met each week. Several different trustees would tell me when I spoke to them privately that I was the face of Stand Against Violence and to give the job to anyone else wouldn't make sense, but whenever we got together as a group they told a different story. One trustee, a friend of mine who was not part of the clique, told me how she thought there was a nasty vibe within the sub-group and she was being frozen out of their meetings. Ben was secretary, and so was not part of the sub-group as this would also have been seen as a conflict of interests. It became clear that the newest member was the ringleader, and she'd been putting ideas in the others' heads in her "butter wouldn't melt" manner. She would then come to me and talk about the "feeling in the group," as if she was confiding in me, but looking back now I think she was just trying to stir up trouble. I've never been able to figure out why. I came to dread the whole group meetings, where every one of my suggestions would be disputed and dragged out, to the point where I was beginning to feel like I had no say in the charity I'd worked so hard to establish. It started to make me quite angry.

Once five months had gone by and there was no resolution to the issue of the CEO role I told the board that enough was enough and we had to sort it out. I reiterated why I thought the role was necessary, why I thought that I was the best person for the job, and listed some opportunities we'd missed over the past five months while this was unresolved. I even offered a compromise, saying that I would step down as chairman but not as a trustee if it would help placate their concerns about a conflict of interests. I didn't want to do this as if I stepped down as trustee it meant I would have to be voted back in, and they might be planning to get rid of me. I tried to tell myself that surely things weren't that extreme, but if I was no longer trustee and then there was no funding for the CEO role or if they decided to fire me then where would it leave me? I would have even less say than I already did. My concerns deepened when they started to pick fault with almost everything I did. I was told off for things I said on Facebook, was questioned on every point, and even had to go back to people I planned to work with and say the board had voted against it happening, which was humiliating. I actually became quite depressed about the whole thing.

Eventually, I reached the end of my tether and basically demanded for a decision to be made. The longer this went on the more it was harming us as a charity, and we were unable to move forward. I knew if we carried on like this everything we'd worked for would just fizzle out, and I was not prepared to let that happen. Not for me, not for us, but most importantly of all, not for Lloyd. At a particularly bad-natured meeting, I was told that they'd come to a decision.

"Okay, Adam," their spokesperson began. "We've decided that you can apply for the job, but only if you step down as a trustee."

"Go on," I said, not quite believing what I was hearing and having the impression that there was more.

"Of course there's no guarantee you will get the job," they continued. "In order to appease Equal Opportunities we'll have to advertise the role, and a more suitable candidate may be interviewed."

I was absolutely livid. Furthermore, this was just the latest in a line of decisions they'd made that led to us losing people who had so much to offer. I have no doubt that if I hadn't stood up to them I would no longer be part of Stand Against Violence today. Rather than describing a worst-case scenario, they were basically telling me that I would be leaving and outlining their exact plan of how it would happen. I should have seen the signs as we'd already lost an excellent teacher. The lady I'd originally asked to help us develop a lesson plan and workshop was treated very unfairly. I'd put forward the idea of employing her, reasoning that if we could pay her to deliver workshops for us it would give security to both her and us, and we could develop our strategy for workshops going forward. We'd know we had someone who was dedicated and very proficient in delivering the work. I even figured out the costings and proposed how we would fund her role. The board dithered over the issue for months, coming back with one concern after another, few of which I understood. This went on for so long that she had no option but to look for work elsewhere. She'd been extremely keen to work with us but she had to earn a living, and because the decision was dragged out we lost her. I was quite upset about this, seeing as she'd helped us from day one, and I was determined that we should repay her support and faith in us by making her a paid employee. Now it seemed they were trying to make me quit by putting one obstacle after another in my way until it became too much.

There wasn't a chance of that happening, and my suspicions about the board's wishes were confirmed when I did my own research and found that they didn't have to advertise for the role. They could have just employed me with a simple e-mail to the charity commission. I knew I had to fight for my place in the charity, but it wasn't long before I had a valuable ally. Once she was on my side there was a massive turning point.

A lady from London applied to be on the board of trustees. Her connection to the area was through a local charity who were focused around the South-West. I went to the board and their response was predictably negative. They asked why someone would want to travel down from London for meetings, but I argued that the fact she was willing to do so showed amazing dedication and that we had to give her a chance. For once they couldn't really argue and so they told me I could interview her and then make a decision. I invited her down and we seemed to get on straight away. We had a lengthy discussion and she seemed perfect for the board in my eyes, so I went back and told the others I wanted her to become a trustee.

"Not yet," said the ringleader, "I think we all need to interview her as a group as well."

I was exasperated by this, as it went totally against what they'd said before, and I was embarrassed to have to tell her she would have to be interviewed again when I'd basically told her she was in. I was convinced she would be put off during the second interview, which was more of an interrogation from the negative element of the board on her motives for travelling so far to be involved with our charity. She didn't bat an eyelid and calmly explained everything she'd said to me before, which impressed me even more. The board were still hesitant, but we took a vote and there were an equal number for and against, which meant that my vote would make all the difference.

She joined our team, if you could call it that at the time, and the dynamic changed straight away. She was very perceptive and didn't mince her words, so she spotted what was going on with the ringleader straight away. She mentioned it to me and I told her everything. Luckily, she agreed with me on many points, and now the majority had swung just slightly in my favour, which really wound up those who remained part of the clique. They became even more argumentative at meetings and if they didn't get their own way, which they usually didn't nowadays, they sat in moody silence like spoilt children.

I felt conflicted, hating that the charity had come to this, but relieved that I no longer felt ousted. I decided to try and refocus on what we were aiming for, and at the next meeting I asked if our trustees could commit to attending two events each per year in order to spread the workload. Our new addition to the board had been doing this already, and at her own expense, which was really helping to ease the pressure on me.

"No, I don't think I can," said the ringleader, "I don't have the time to spare on top of the monthly meetings."

"Two days a year isn't much, though, surely?" said our new board member. "It's not fair on Adam having to attend everything when he already works full-time. Surely we can all help him out a little bit?"

The ringleader went silent, as did the others who had refused. The next day she called me.

"I'm sorry, Adam, but I feel I have no option but to step down," she said. "I've spoken to the others and our feeling is that the organisation isn't going in the right direction."

"I'm sorry to hear that but I understand your decision," I said.

I wasn't particularly sorry in her case if I'm brutally honest, as I felt she'd been the one who instigated all of the problems. Two more stepped down soon afterwards, though, and I was a little upset because they'd both been great supporters of what I was trying to achieve in the early days. The treasurer was a particularly sad loss because a good treasurer is hard to find. However, she did agree to stay in the role until we found a replacement. I really appreciated this kind gesture, especially after all that had gone on, and within a couple of months, we'd found two people who wanted to share the role after one had changed their mind before starting. Sadly, my friend who'd been treated coldly at the sub-group meetings also left, because the negative atmosphere at the meetings had made her feel disillusioned over time. I knew we would have to find replacements who were truly dedicated and would not reignite the dysfunctional mood of before. With that in mind, we asked one of our long-standing volunteers to become a board member, and she was delighted to agree. We also asked my mum, which of course would be a conflict of interests as she would be biased towards me, but we all seemed to be on the same page now anyway and so I didn't see this causing conflict.

The bitter, unproductive rows the meetings had become were replaced with lively, productive discussions that helped us to move the charity forward rather than sinking us in quicksand. Everyone mucked in so we were able to have a presence at more events and people saw us as a collective rather than a one-man crusade. For the first time in quite a while, I was able to look to the future with enthusiasm and ambition rather than constantly wondering where it had all gone wrong with the charity. I later asked the teacher if she would come back but understandably she'd moved on by now and so we'd lost her for good. I vowed I would never make such a mistake again.

The new board is fantastic and is made up of dedicated individuals who are skilled in different areas that are all vital to the organisation as a whole. A few have come and gone since that dreadful time, but we've never had such an unpleasant atmosphere since. I am so thankful to the original board members for all they did to help the charity, and I don't believe they would have been so difficult if the ringleader hadn't come in and shaken things up. Maybe it needed to happen in order for us to move forward.

Our trustee from London remained a dedicated member of the team throughout, proving that those who opposed her early on only did so out of petulance. What I was most thrilled about on a personal level was that the new board voted unanimously to employ me as the CEO. We secured six months' funding for this to happen and they trusted that I had the necessary skills and experience to make a success of the role, not to mention that I had started the campaign which became the charity. My enthusiasm and drive for it were stronger than ever. The previous board had wanted me to do a management course. That was when they even considered me taking on the role.

An e-mail was sent to the charity commission and that was that. I reduced my hours at the hospital and was able to dedicate heaps of time to the charity. I would even be able to have a little time to myself, and time on my own no longer seemed like an ordeal. Enough years had passed since Lloyd's death for the most intense waves of grief to have subsided.

I was so excited, but I knew it was time to think of some new ideas because I was now just a little too old to be considered a "young person" by 02. This meant the opportunities through them dried up. However, being involved with their programme had allowed me to grow so much both personally and professionally. The dreadful experiences with the board threatened to undo all of that good work, but my new role as CEO gave me renewed belief, and I knew I had the backing of the trustees to aim for new heights.

Jay: Five

The average prison, in my experience, isn't very supportive towards change. It was only when I was moved to Grendon, near Aylesbury in Buckinghamshire, that I started to properly face up to what I had caused. That was what led to me becoming who I am today. Grendon is a really supportive place, where you are actually given a chance to look at the person you were when you came to prison and think about whether that's who you truly are, or who you want to be. I can say for sure that I'm a different person now to the kid I was when I stood trial. I don't have the same anger I had then, and my outlook on life has completely changed. I'm nothing like I was then. I do consider myself to be a very different person.

It wasn't just getting older that changed my attitude. What I was able to do in Grendon they would call rehabilitation, but I just look at it as changing myself as a person, through realising who I had become and deciding who I wanted to be. I won't tell you everything I talked about in those sessions, and is it fair that I got the chance to become who I am today when Lloyd never did? Of course not, but that's the one thing I will never be able to change. Now I'm going to tell you what happened in my life up until that moment.

From an early age, my happiest memories were always about sport and being out and about. I grew up in Lowestoft in Suffolk and was always going to summer football camps. I even went to Holland to play one year.

There were some really good times, and I was always happy when I was out kicking a ball around.

I come from quite a big family. My mum has two sisters with three kids each and we would always be around each other's houses, which I always enjoyed. My aunties' families are more like I wish mine had been. I'm the oldest of three brothers, and my dad was never around. The others had "normal" families with a mum and a dad, and they seemed happy, but I never got jealous or acted nasty towards them.

My mum met another lady who had three kids. She became friends with my mum, and her kids became friends of mine. I was out and about with one of them one day when I was about ten or eleven, and he took a stereo out of a van while I acted as the lookout. We got arrested really quickly. I didn't know what was going on, but that was the first time I remember being in trouble. I don't think I was an especially bad kid, but I did get up to mischief and this was the first time I got caught.

I always knew the difference between right and wrong, and I knew what I did wasn't right, but I didn't really get punished for it, so I didn't see it as a starting point for going down the wrong path in life. My dad wasn't around and so I didn't have a big scary man to tell me off. I was a little bit lawless already, but I think I tried to justify getting in trouble by telling myself I was only standing at the edge of a car park and I hadn't been the one who stole the stereo.

I liked my life in Lowestoft. I had friends, I could play football all the time, which I really enjoyed, and there was plenty of family nearby. It was quite a happy community really, and I never really felt like my life was difficult. I understand now that my mum was in a horrible relationship with an abusive man. Sometimes she was so scared that she'd get me out of bed to sit with her in the middle of the night because she knew he wouldn't hit her if I was sat there. It never really made sense to me at the time, and one day she just packed some things in a suitcase and we left, so she could escape him. I didn't really understand, and so I was just angry that she was taking me away from all my friends and family. My view of the world was very materialistic, because I was so young, and I think that's where I developed my attitude. Looking back now, she could have lost her life if she'd stuck around and she was getting away from a dangerous situation. I wish I could have appreciated this at the time.

We moved all over the place at the beginning, around a lot of different council estates, from Eastleigh to Southampton, to Bridgwater and then to Taunton. When we moved so often it was hard to maintain friendships, and so I became quite angry and anti-social. We moved around Taunton quite a bit too, but at least we were in the same town and I was able to start forming some friendships there. Football was still my thing, and I started to play every weekend again. It was what I looked forward to all week at school.

I knew quite a lot of people, and I guess I was fairly popular through the football and skating communities, then when I got a bit older I would go drinking in the park at weekends, so I was quite well known. The people I was hanging out with on the night Lloyd died had a reputation for fighting, which they had created themselves. Not everyone I hung out with was like that, but that particular group were definitely known for violence and were known to the police already. I would say they were friends of mine, but I was closest to the guys who weren't actually involved in the main fight, and I definitely didn't see myself as someone who was always looking for trouble. I never really got in fights usually, but I had a lot of anger and would sometimes end up punching a wall in frustration or something like that. Some of that group had ASBOs already, and they were being monitored by the police. I didn't have a reputation like they did.

When I was coming towards the end of my time at Ladymead School, I hung out with that group quite a lot. I went to a number of different schools, and I was never very academic. I saw school more as a place I would go to chill with a few friends rather than to learn. I was one of the youngest in my year and hadn't yet turned sixteen when I left, but instead of going on to college or anything like that, I went straight into work. I was spending less and less time with the lads I grew up with on the estate. I was working in the week and playing football at weekends, so I was busier than I used to be. I don't know why I chose to go to work straight away. I was too young to realise the consequences of my actions and I never really had much of a direction in life. I was only going to work to earn money and was never thinking about what sort of career I might have. When I wasn't at work I was smoking a lot of weed and not really thinking about the future. I was never looking far ahead.

I was working as a wall tiler back in 2005. My mum had sorted this out through a resource centre in Priorswood and then I got passed on to an older guy who had his own business. He lived just round the corner and took me under his wing, training me up. We were getting on well, but then his partner's son came into the fold and there was tension between us from the start. One day I called the guy up and said I wasn't coming.

"I need you," he said. "You have to come."

"No, I'm not coming."

"If you don't come today I'm afraid you haven't got a job anymore."

I called his bluff, but he was as good as his word and I lost the job. That could have been a really good opportunity, but I messed it up because of my poor attitude. I was an angry kid with no direction and I'd made a stupid decision. I remember feeling afterwards like I'd really messed up, which didn't help me feel any less angry. Soon after that, I got in a fight and a young man died because of it. I was charged with murder and sentenced to 12 years in prison. If you'd not known that last bit about me and read my story up until that point without knowing where I ended up would you ever have guessed? I never thought for a second I would end up in prison. I just wasn't that kind of lad.

When most people think of a murderer they think of a cold-blooded killer with a twisted mind. I knew I wasn't a monster, but in Grendon, for the first time, I was able to look in the mirror and admit to what I'd done. I know that Lloyd died because of me. I know that because of what I did his life was wasted, and his family was torn apart. I will never try and make excuses for that. The fact is that there was always potential for someone to get hurt because of me. I never thought any fight would go that far, and I definitely never meant for anyone to die, but that is what I caused.

When my parole hearing was in sight I started to think a lot more about

Lloyd's family and I learnt that his brother, Adam, had started a charity. The idea came to me, as I continued to look at changing myself as a person, that maybe someday he would want to talk to me about what happened, and I was willing to do that. I had no idea how he might feel towards me. I'm pretty sure if it was the other way round, I'd have hated him, but maybe I would have wanted to know why it happened. I lied in court, and I felt like he deserved to know the truth, but would he want to hear it? I put the idea to my parole officer and at first I was told it wasn't a good idea, but it was something I just couldn't forget. I wanted him to know how sorry I was, and if it would help him to hear everything I truly remembered about the night Lloyd died then I would answer any questions he might have. I hoped that one day I would at least be able to offer him the chance, whether he said yes or no.

Making It Professional

I f it hadn't been for what happened to Lloyd, I almost certainly wouldn't have ended up counting violence prevention among my personal interests, but setting up a charity with this as the main aim made it almost inevitable. It occurred to me over the years that the bigger the charity got the more important it became for me to know what I was talking about. At the beginning, my talks had focused solely on Lloyd's story, and of course this was still what I based them around, but as I became more clued up on facts and figures to do with violence I started to incorporate more and more of them, and the talks became informative as well as emotive. Nowadays I can answer pretty much any question on the topic with confidence, but it took a long time and a whole lot of research to get there.

I began to read a lot of research papers on violence, and through this I spoke to some academics who had studied the topic extensively. There was one doctor from Liverpool John Moores University who had written a paper explicitly on violence prevention. I made contact with her and she took a genuine interest in my work, as I had in hers, and we began to communicate regularly. She directed me to the World Health Organisation's data on the subject, and I began to feel a lot more knowledgeable; that I had proper, informed answers at my fingertips when anyone questioned what I said.

Those who had mentored me early on began to refer to me as a specialist and a consultant in violence prevention. At first I almost laughed this off, thinking "You old charmers!" but as time went on and I learnt more and more I came to realise that this was basically true. Over a number of years, I had accrued enough knowledge and experience that people could actually learn from me about the subject as well as me learning from others. It was a strange feeling, but it did my self-esteem no harm, and it meant other individuals and organisations had more respect for me, whereas at the beginning they may have admired me and felt sympathy because of my story but certainly didn't see me as any kind of authority on violence prevention.

What we understood about Lloyd's killers and other perpetrators of violent crime was that young people often lacked understanding of the consequences of violence, and how one snap decision could change their lives forever. Technology had moved on once again since we'd made the original film back in 2008. It was changing rapidly, and now in 2013 there were far more possibilities that had never existed before. I had plans to develop this aspect further and so I reconnected with the original filmmaker; he'd been kind enough to help me out for free originally, and so it only seemed right to get him involved again but this time to pay him for his work. I knew we shared a similar vision and could work well together. I told him I was looking to create a new film that embraced the possibilities of new technology and he jumped at the chance to get involved.

We wanted to create a resource for young people that highlighted the importance of making the right decisions. The idea was to create an interactive film, in the style of Bear Grylls' *You vs. Wild* series if you've seen it (this was a long time before that series existed but it makes a good comparison in terms of the interactive aspect.) Basically, the film would play in segments, and then the viewers would be able to make decisions and link to different segments based on what they chose to do, then they would be shown the outcome.

At first we perhaps got a little carried away with the possibilities of new technology, as I wanted to make this a virtual reality experience. The filmmaker was on board with the idea, and he even designed a prototype headset that you could play films on (this was before the days of the first commercial VR headsets), as well as recording on. He invited me to test it out, and I was absolutely blown away. I felt like I was in a different world, and was actually inside the film, walking around and experiencing it for real rather than just watching it on a screen. It was incredible and it was actually quite scary how real it seemed! When I started to think about everything more logistically I pictured 30 kids with headsets stumbling around a classroom and bumping into each other. Aside from having the potential for mishaps, the VR would make it quite an isolating experience, whereas we were trying to encourage collective learning. We wanted discussions within the classes about violence prevention. Also, making it VR would mean the cost would be huge, which wouldn't be very sustainable.

After discussing everything in depth we decided to make it a 3D interactive film instead and applied to the Home Office Innovations Fund for the capital to make it happen. I wasn't sure they would go for it, especially as we'd asked for two years' worth of funding, so I was absolutely delighted when I received confirmation that they were going to give us every penny! I told the filmmaker the good news and we were in a jubilant mood, getting to work straight away. Because of the interactive element, it was a complicated script, and the planning stage took a lot longer than the previous film had. Instead of me just writing everything out when I woke up in the middle of the night we figured everything out together over a number of lengthy meetings. Luckily, I was able to dedicate some of my working hours to the project this time, otherwise it would have meant a lot of very late nights!

Once the plan was firmly in place we couldn't have been more excited to get going, and we threw ourselves into the production. I should have been prepared for a spanner to be thrown in the works, but I was just too caught up in everything to consider any setbacks. A few days into production I received a call from one of our funders.

"Now," he began after introducing himself, "I'm sorry to tell you there has been an error."

Oh, no! What now?

"Because the list was in alphabetical order we hadn't noticed there was a problem with your application at first, but we've discovered that we've awarded funding to too many projects, and so there isn't actually enough money left for you to receive the amount we originally stated."

"But we've already begun work on the project," I said, beginning to panic. "Are you saying there's no funding whatsoever?"

"Oh, no," he quickly reassured me. "But we will have to ask you to reapply for the first year's funding. We can cover 12 months, but I'm afraid we won't be able to fund you beyond that."

This was pretty dreadful news, and I wasn't convinced we'd be able to go ahead with the project at all. As I thought about it further it seemed quite frightening that such an error could be made over something so important and that there was nothing we could do about it. I knew it was pointless to dispute the error and insist they had to pay us what was originally agreed, because if the money wasn't there then it wasn't there. Besides, I had been in this game long enough to know that setbacks happen all the time. You just have to keep calm and carry on.

I reapplied and we did receive some money, but to make such an ambitious film on a much lower budget was something I wasn't sure would be possible. We decided to proceed, and the original enthusiasm, especially after the funding debacle, was replaced with a sombre atmosphere when we were faced with the realities of such a complex project. Without wishing to get too technical, the film was going to be shot in first-person so it seemed like the viewer was actually experiencing the events, and while the camera was constantly moving it was difficult to pinpoint the convergence points that were necessary to create the 3D effect. This became very time-consuming. It was such a laborious task. Then we discovered what using the voting technology that allowed the film to be interactive would entail. We'd been assured it could be integrated into the project, but then we found out that we would need a "developer license" to make it happen, which would give the company exclusive rights. Rights that could, in theory, be revoked at any time. I pictured this happening on the day before the launch, and it wasn't a risk we could take, so we had to look at other options.

I approached a local IT company to see if they could offer a solution, and it was complicated but sounded workable. They would custom-build a computer framework that could hold the clips and link them together, then the interactive element could be accessed through a wireless network using tablet PCs. At times it felt like we should have stuck with the good old traditional film setup because the more ambitious an idea is, the more complex the whole thing becomes and the more potential there is for something to go wrong. Things did go wrong frequently, and I began to wonder if we'd made a terrible mistake. The filming and editing ended up being the smoothest part of the process, and it was the technology that linked everything together we had most issues with. We bought the tablets through a company that kept sending us refurbished units that didn't seem up to the job. Obviously, this was frustrating, and even at the launch event half of the tablets either lost connection or stopped working altogether, which was pretty embarrassing. Overall the launch could be considered a success in the end though.

I decided to try and cement relations with the local police while the filming was going on. After a new head was appointed at the local station I had found relations to be a lot better, and so I thought it was the perfect time to try and move on from the difficulties of the past. I was still quite sceptical, and when I asked them to be involved in the film, I was bracing myself for a list of conditions but was pleasantly surprised when they agreed to take part with no strings attached. Their only request was that the ID numbers on their police badges weren't visible on the film, and this was no issue whatsoever. The two officers who got involved with the film were pleasant to work with. They were enthusiastic and helpful. I couldn't have asked for more.

When it came to the launch event the police chief superintendent came along with the two officers who had been involved in the film. Also the youth offending leads, who were still quite sceptical about us, decided to give us another chance. I asked one of my academic colleagues to come along and make a speech about violence in the UK as part of a joint presentation with me. Our aim was to highlight, through statistics as well as personal stories, the need for our work due to violence still being a significant issue in the South-West. I thought it was an emotive and professional presentation that put the message of the film across in a broader context. It wasn't intended to belittle the work of any other organisation, more to explain how we all needed to work together to tackle the issue, but sadly the police once again seemed to take it personally. After I spoke to a few people afterwards I noticed that the police superintendent and my academic colleague had both vanished.

I caught up with my academic colleague soon afterwards and she said that she'd received quite an ear-bashing from the police, which I think upset her a little bit. Shortly afterwards one of the inspectors came over to me and after complimenting me on the evening and on the resource he said he would send me some more up-to-date statistics as mine were not accurate. I told him exactly where they had come from and assured him that my sources were reputable. He said he'd never heard of them and that I should only be using the crime survey stats. After briefly going round in circles we agreed to disagree on the matter and everything was still amicable.

I'd forgotten about it and was pleased at how well the launch event had gone despite the technical hitches. We'd decided between us not to carry on the argument, and so it made me quite angry when I received an e-mail a few days later from the same inspector telling me that he'd discussed my sources with the superintendent and they agreed that my statistics were wildly inaccurate. I would have just not responded but I felt it was unnecessary to have sent me the e-mail, and I believed that they were wrong, so I took a little time and e-mailed several different authorities, one being a statistician at the ONS, one of my inaccurate data sources, about the statistics, explaining everything that had happened. They all mentioned the phrase "wildly inaccurate" in their replies, saying that this was quite a bold claim.

I did my research into the crime survey, which the police insisted should be my only source, and I discovered that it's a random survey of 40,000 people across the UK in which those who answer give their opinions on crime and how safe they feel on the whole. Although you would think that this is enough people to build up a reasonably accurate picture of peoples' feelings on crime it's still quite a small fraction of the 60 million people in the UK. A lot must get left out. I had also known for a long time that many violent crimes go unreported, so I knew that I needed to look at more sources in order to build up a full picture of the extent of violent crime in the UK.

I can understand why the police would want to use the results of the crime survey, but to discount all other sources just seemed needlessly ignorant. I wished they would accept that it was never my intention to show them in a poor light. I was merely speaking the truth about violence and highlighting the need for extra resources to deal with the problem. Of course I would love to believe that violence isn't an issue, and it would be wonderful if we lived in a society where nobody suffers violent attacks, but I know that the reality is different. I'm living proof that these incidents do go on, and that the consequences can be tragic. My research has told me that I'm far from being the only one who has suffered in this way, and so I won't speak anything but the truth in my presentations. The issue of violence will never go away if we pretend it's not there in order to make everything appear rosy. The attitude of the police on this one matter always frustrated me, but things were becoming more amicable over time and nowadays I would say we have a good relationship. I put together a polite and friendly reply to the e-mail, but made it clear I didn't agree and included various statistics to back up my point. I never got a reply.

I knew that not everyone in the police held the same opinion, and I was able to build a good relationship with some other forces. We'd begun to work with the schools' officers in the local cities, and they found our film to be a valuable resource. Nobody said we were scaremongering. I even began to deliver some workshops alongside officers in some of the schools. Despite this, I did become quite paranoid at times about the police in my own town. At one point I even worried that they might try and start a campaign against me, which would discredit the work we were doing, or even that they might be monitoring my home! These suspicions proved to be unfounded, and I was delighted when the Youth Offending Team decided to give us another chance and we ran some pilot workshops with young offenders. They couldn't deny the positive impact the workshops had and admitted there was reduced reoffending over time, even though they never wanted to let us take the credit. The only change on their programme had been to involve us again . . . just saying.

For some reason, we were still finding it difficult to get a lot of schools to engage with us. We made a concerted effort in this area and did see our bookings double, but this was not enough. Around half of the schools in the region still wouldn't have us in, and so that was a lot of young people we were unable to engage with. Having said that, all of the schools who had us in rebooked, and so we knew our workshops were effective. We tried different tactics to reach those who seemed less keen to have us in. As part of this, I tried to get booked in to talk at various meetings of head teachers and PSHE teachers. A couple of these had gone very well and the teachers all seemed enthusiastic, but none of their schools booked us and so it seemed to have been a waste of time.

I met with a lady from the Healthy Schools Team and was confident that this would be a way in, but she seemed quite negative towards the film.

"We've seen various shock tactics used, which are proven to be ineffective," she said. "And I'm afraid we see your film as just another example of this."

"Have you actually seen the film?" I asked, not understanding how she could have that opinion.

"No."

I was stunned. She didn't even look embarrassed to have admitted it.

"How can you have a judgement on the film when you've not even seen it?" I asked. "We've had a lot of great feedback from schools who have taken part in the workshops, and most of them have us back. It's your job to inform schools of resources, but how can you do that if you've not even seen them?"

"Okay," she sighed. "I doubt the teachers will go for it but you're welcome to come and speak at our next meeting."

I found her attitude to be ridiculous, and I thought it must be informed by some kind of prejudice, but I was excited to have the opportunity to speak at the meeting, and I found that all of the teachers who attended were impressed with the film.

"We've actually been using this as a resource over the past year," said one of them. "We weren't sure if the content was suitable but we asked our pupils for their opinion. They agreed that it was hard-hitting but also that it was something they needed to see. I would have no hesitation in recommending this to any school."

It was almost as if I'd paid him to be at the meeting and told him what to say! It was quite unbelievable really, but I had the same experience at another meeting I attended. This still didn't generate any bookings, which was perplexing and quite maddening, but at least I knew the film was being seen in some schools we hadn't actually been to. This meant our message was getting to more people than we had realised, which was encouraging.

Many times people have told us that our prices are too low, so maybe people think that low cost will equate to low quality. Others have told us we're too expensive, so who knows really? Some organisations charge £1,000 for a workshop and seem to generate a lot of bookings. This is way more than we charge, so it's just a case of persistence.

Part of our difficulty has been that schools are busy, their curriculums are tight and PSHE, which is where we usually fit in, is not compulsory. We're not the only organisation who are trying to fit into their schedule; far from it, and so when someone else gets in touch trying to take up another slice of their time it must feel quite stressful. It's an area we've been persistent in, as schools are one of the best places to reach our main target audience. What we are hoping is that if enough young people are educated about the impact of violence and its possible effects then a gradual generational change will occur. It's hard to imagine that violence will just disappear as an issue altogether, but if people realise at a young age that it can ruin lives then a lot of families might avoid what we went through. This has been our aim all along.

We realised that in order to reach more schools we would need a member of staff who could focus on this alone. We had taken one of our dedicated volunteers on in an admin role, and a big part of this became marketing to schools. Since a targeted effort has been made in this area we have seen a definite improvement, but it remains a challenge. Obviously, we would love for our workshops to be a permanent part of the curriculum in every school every year. This still seems a long way off, but we are moving in the right direction. As always, money is part of the problem, but we have eased the concerns on our side by utilising freelance teachers to deliver the workshops, so if a booking is made the school pay, and then the teacher's fee is covered. Sometimes we are also able to obtain grant funding to target schools in a certain area. A lot of schools have a limited budget for workshops and so it can be hard to get them to agree. This problem would be solved if the government focused more of their attention on preparing kids for life, as well as for exams.

This is one area of education that I feel is really lacking. With PSHE not being a compulsory part of the curriculum, young people are missing out on vital life lessons. You might say these are the responsibility of the parents, but time in school should be about a rounded education that will help prepare pupils for life as well as to get them the qualifications that will help them to find employment. If young people are unprepared for the different aspects of adult life then how are they meant to cope with all of the various demands that they don't have to as a child. Life skills programmes have been proven to reduce risk factors for violence.

There is a lot less emphasis on building character than there used to be, and I think all of these things that are lacking in modern education rob young people of important coping strategies, as well as a better chance of becoming fully rounded individuals. This is something I feel our workshops help to provide, along with numerous others from excellent organisations who are trying to get bookings in schools. A lot of children grow up with a lack of respect and empathy for others, and there are many reasons for this, but I truly believe that more of an emphasis on PSHE would be a help.

With it being unknown how many schools will want to have us in at the time of writing due to the Coronavirus, it remains to be seen how frequently we will be able to offer workshops for the foreseeable future. However, we have recently developed a virtual workshop as a new way of getting our message across. In December 2018 we delivered a workshop to home-educated children for the first time, and we would definitely do this again if anyone wanted to book us.

Many schools say they have a zero-tolerance approach to bullying, and our workshops could not be more in line with this message. We show what the impact of violence can be, and why the decisions we make in this regard can have huge implications. If someone learns this at an early age they are more likely to consider the impact of violence as they grow up. I keep reiterating this message, but it just makes perfect sense that schools should have us in. We are yet to find the perfect approach that will convince all of them about the necessity of our work, but we will persevere.

The year before the pandemic, we had educated over 38,000 young people across England and Wales. Ninety-six percent of them claimed to have changed their attitudes towards violence, stating they were less likely to resort to violence as a means of conflict resolution following our workshop. That's over 36,000 young people who are safer as a result of our work in a single year.

Achievements and Opportunities

In 2014, my royalist heart was thumping when we applied for the Queen's Award for the voluntary sector. This isn't an award you are nominated for, but there is a lengthy application process, and if you are recommended they add you to a shortlist, from which you can be chosen as a winner. I received a voicemail from an extremely well-spoken man who introduced himself simply as "Brigadier" and wanted me to call him back to discuss our application. I was nervous. I've never considered myself to be posh, and I recalled the "what violence?" comment of the upper-class gentleman way back in the days of the petition, wondering if the brigadier would be similarly oblivious to the issue. I called him, preparing myself for confused silences as I explained what we were about before he politely declined to take us any further. It was the Deputy Lord-Lieutenant of Somerset I would be speaking to, and I began, "Hello, Brigadier . . ."

"Please, call me by my first name," he said in a friendly tone. This put me at ease straight away and we had a great chat. He seemed very impressed with the work we had done and ended the call by telling me he would have no hesitation in recommending us for the award. We would hear in due course if we were to be lucky recipients.

I was very encouraged by the conversation. I tried not to get my hopes up too much but I was excited all the same. The weeks went by and I always rushed to the letterbox when the mail came but then weeks became months and there was nothing, so I accepted that we had been unsuccessful. I had completely forgotten about the whole thing, then one day much later a letter arrived telling us that we had won. There was an invitation to the Queen's Garden Party at Buckingham Palace for me and a few guests. I had a smile on my face for the rest of that day.

I've always admired the royal family for their entire lives of dedication and service, and I see them as an historical asset to the nation. Ben, my mum and one of our trustees would join me for the occasion. Now the day had arrived my excitement turned to nerves. I couldn't get an old episode of Mr. Bean out of my head where he met the Queen and accidentally headbutted her by bowing too vigorously! If the CEO of Stand Against Violence was to assault the Queen the tabloid press would feel like all of their Christmases had come at once, and the headlines would follow me round for the rest of my life. I felt so paranoid.

I reasoned that I was probably being silly because it was unlikely I would even meet her. Right back at the beginning of the campaign, I'd been convinced I was going to meet Tony Blair when we went to deliver the petitions, but that never happened. When we arrived and saw the huge gathering of guests it seemed even less likely. I was pretty disappointed, but within minutes a man with a top hat and tails approached us holding an umbrella and struck up a conversation.

"Would you like to meet the Queen?" he asked me.

"Yes, please!" I said straight away.

I tried to make my reply sound as casual as possible, not wanting him to change his mind about the offer if I seemed a little too enthusiastic. I couldn't contain my excitement and felt like Lloyd was with us once again. The chain of events that led to me being here was set in motion when he was attacked, and of course I would have traded this opportunity and all of those that had come before to have him back, but it would be in his cheeky spirit to tell him "Thanks for what you went through to let me meet Her Majesty. Best brother ever!"

As a group of us were gathered together the Mr. Bean episode resurfaced, and I had no idea how I was meant to address her, the correct way to bow or anything. My throat went a little dry. We were escorted by the

Queen's beefeaters, who cleared a path through the crowds and led us to a walkway, where we all lined up to receive Her Majesty. We were briefed on how to address her but were told not to worry about slipping up as the Queen was very easy to talk to, so we should just be ourselves. This was easier said than done, and none of us could help feeling nervous. Before we knew it the national anthem began to play and we looked around to see that various members of the royal family had appeared. I would have loved to have met Will, Kate or Harry as well, as they were of a similar age to me, but you can't have everything. Harry was, of course, still very much part of the royal scene back then and I'm not sure if he and Meghan had even met.

When I first saw the Queen standing at the top of the palace steps on the huge patio I was quite surprised by how short she was. I guess she's getting on a bit and we all shrink as we get older, but even I would tower over her. She was dressed in yellow and was instantly recognisable. When the anthem finished, she began to greet the different groups, and we were quite far back in the line. I'm not sure if we were in alphabetical order. It was quite an anxious wait, and the sense of anticipation was huge. When she eventually got to us we were all introduced, and we managed to address her in the correct way with a bow or curtsey. So far, so good. Then she asked me what we had won the award for and I lost the ability to form a sentence. Various words came out of my mouth in no particular relevant order, and she probably suspected that English was not my first language. At least I didn't say "I'm sorry, ma'am. I can't form a sentence because I'm terrified I might accidentally headbutt you!"

I managed to compose myself and tried again, this time at least making partial sense.

"I can't believe the problems there are with violence nowadays," the Queen said to me. "Work like yours is most definitely necessary."

I couldn't believe it. Not only had the Queen spoken to me directly but she had actually listened to what I said and validated all of the hard work I'd been doing over a number of years now. The Queen gets bad press from some people, but she was over 80 years old and still made the effort to engage with a number of different people, showing the same level of interest in each conversation. She wasn't on her phone planning her next speech when we were talking. I had her full attention, and she didn't tell me that my view on the level of violence in the nation she reigned over was misguided. She accepted that there was a problem with violence in the UK and told me that my work was important in trying to address it. She stayed mentally switched on throughout, which I sometimes struggle with even in my thirties! I thought she was incredible, and I even managed not to headbutt her. If I had it would probably have made her change her mind about me. Phew!

I will never forget that experience, and to have had that kind of recognition from her when a number of politicians, police officers, teachers, and others over the years had tried to discredit my work gave me more determination than ever to keep going. I had been on the violence prevention campaign trail for nearly ten years now, and I wanted to continue. I felt like I had a lifelong commitment to Lloyd, but this had become so much bigger now than just my story. The Queen's Award was an honour not just for me but for everyone who had been a part of Stand Against Violence from the original campaign up until now. We received the actual award later on that year, but I hadn't realised it was up to us to arrange the presentation evening until quite near the time. This meant the whole thing was put together in a rush, and I wasn't convinced many would be able to attend. I was hoping, realistically, for about 10. I was especially pessimistic about numbers because the Lord-Lieutenant of Somerset, who would be presenting the award, had said that my intended time of 7.30pm was too late. I wanted it to be at this time so people didn't have to rush there straight from work. Several of our trustees were unable to attend but it worked better for the majority of people, so 6pm it was.

Around 30 people made it to the Council Chambers to hear me make a brief speech, which was followed by the presentation. The Lord-Lieutenant was fantastic. I'd met her once before at the magistrates' AGM, and she seemed very supportive of our work. I caught up with my mum afterwards.

"The Lord-Lieutenant seemed genuinely pleased to be presenting the award," she told me. "She looked very happy all evening."

"I thought so too," I said. "I hope she was because she knows some influential people. She would be a powerful ally!"

My mum smiled. I am genuinely so grateful for all of her and Dad's belief and support since I began the campaign. I really hope I've made them proud.

"Did you see that policeman though?" she added.

"What do you mean?"

"He pursed his lips when you read out the statistics!"

"Ha! Some things never change."

We laughed about this. You've got to really, haven't you? I did have another reason to smile that evening though. There were two policemen there: one I knew and one I had never met. The one I knew had been very supportive of us in the past, and I felt like I knew him well enough to ask about the e-mail I'd sent to his superintendent before.

"Oh yeah, that was definitely received," he said.

"I hope he wasn't too offended?" I asked.

"Well, what I can tell you is that he checked all of your sources and admitted that you were right."

Let's just say it wasn't the worst news I'd ever heard. I knew I'd been right all along, but I was delighted that the police superintendent knew it too. I have a good relationship with the police nowadays, which is what I wanted from the start. I know the problems some officers had with me weren't shared by the whole force. It would be the same with any organisation; not everyone holds the same views.

The Queen's Award came after another somewhat different instance of high-profile support. I received an e-mail one day from Laura, one of our dedicated volunteers. She couldn't contain her excitement and told me I wouldn't believe it but she thought she had snared us a celebrity ambassador.

The full story was that she had been bought tickets for a comedy show at The Brewhouse Theatre in Taunton featuring Paul Sinha, aka "The

Sinnerman" from ITV's popular quiz show "The Chase." She wasn't really familiar with his work outside of the show, and so didn't know what to expect, but thought she would go along. After he walked on stage and introduced himself as a "Ranked quizmaster, stand-up comedian and GP" he kept her and her plus one laughing non-stop, and when he announced that he would be in the foyer afterwards if anyone wanted to chat they were very keen to meet him. After they had been talking to him for a little while he asked, "Where's the place to go in Taunton on a Thursday night?"

Reasoning that they might never have a chance to go for a drink with "The Sinnerman" again, they invited him to join them at Okoko, Taunton's premier nightspot . . . admittedly, this isn't saying much. After the drinks began to flow Laura told him a little about Stand Against Violence. Like the Queen had with me, he listened intently and seemed genuinely interested. He asked a number of questions, and Laura told him about the work we did in schools, and some stalls she'd manned for us at festivals. The more she told him the more she realised that his interest went beyond politeness, and the conversation went on for a long time. She was stunned when he gave her a business card at the end of the night and said "Contact me tomorrow. I'd love to get involved. Maybe I could be an ambassador?"

When she got home she e-mailed me straight away. It was the next day before I saw it, but I re-read it several times, thinking "Yes, Laura! You genius!" We had been looking for a celebrity supporter for some time but were keen to find someone who had a genuine passion for our work rather than an arrangement through their manager to voice their support. It seemed that the moment had arrived, but I was nervous about making a fool of myself when I spoke to Paul and unravelling all of Laura's excellent work. Nonetheless, I knew I had to bite the bullet, and so Paul and I arranged to talk over coffee in Wells.

I wasn't worried about headbutting Paul, as I genuinely had been with the Queen, but I was deeply anxious about making a good impression, because I knew how popular a show The Chase was. If such a recognisable and popular man as Paul was to talk about us I felt like people would listen. It was clear from everything Laura had told me that he was already keen to help. Even though my confidence was sky high compared to where it had been when the campaign began, I just couldn't seem to shake the feeling that he might change his mind when he met the "weird" CEO. I'm certain that my belief had its roots in what I went through at primary school, and no matter how much I achieve or how different things are nowadays I just can't seem to shake it off completely. Perhaps I was also a little concerned that Paul would adopt his "Sinnerman" persona and stare at me with an arched eyebrow as I spoke before taking me apart with a series of witty put-downs.

As it happened I needn't have worried. Paul was nothing but friendly from the moment we shook hands and said hello, and it was clear that everything he'd told Laura came from a genuine place. He was very keen to help, and had clearly been thinking about how, as he already had some ideas in mind!

"I can do some posts on social media, to begin with," he said. "I can reach quite a few people on there. Then I'll put together a fundraising night. That would hopefully bring in a helpful amount. Let me have a think and speak to a few people and we'll see what we can come up with."

When he mentioned fundraising I tried not to let him see the pound signs flashing in my eyes. The reality of running a charity is that you have to think about money; it's what enables you to keep the work going. We were trying to develop the community fundraising aspect, as more success there would mean we weren't relying so much on the success of grant applications. We had wages to cover, not just mine, but we now had a paid bookings coordinator, and we were hoping to build up our reserves a little bit so we could fund new projects. The financial climate was changing, and it was becoming harder to make successful bids. We hosted an annual ball that brought in around £1,000 each time, and several of our trustees and volunteers organised some smaller events throughout the year, which brought in around £400 each. This was a valuable contribution, but we were all in agreement that it didn't really reflect the amount of work that everyone put in. With Paul on board, I was hoping we could bring in some more substantial amounts. Our meeting seemed to go well, even though I had said a few things that made me squirm when I recalled them afterwards. Maybe I was just being paranoid again.

A while later Paul came back to me and said he'd reached out to some friends on the comedy circuit, putting together a line-up for a fundraising night at London's Comedy Store. I couldn't believe it. It could be hard enough to get the local council to help, and so for a celebrity who I'd only just met to go out of his way to help us was mind-blowing. All I would have to do was come along and make a speech on the night. I couldn't believe it when he told me the line-up, which included Ed Byrne, Mark Watson, and Romesh Ranganathan, all instantly recognisable from the TV. There was also Daniel Kitson, who I was not so familiar with but was held in very high esteem on the comedy circuit and would be a fantastic addition to the bill. Paul had come up trumps, and we couldn't believe our luck to have him on board. Paul also announced his support on social media, explaining why the cause meant so much to him. He said that he had seen first-hand the extent of the violence problem in the UK, both through his work as a doctor in an A&E department, and from witnessing a number of fights when travelling through city centres on his way to and from stand-up performances. He had even suffered a violent attack in a Glasgow kebab shop on one occasion, so he knew our work was relevant and was proactive in his support from day one.

The icing on the cake was that Paul's manager was behind him 100% in his support for us, and even organised a raffle for the evening. It was such a luxury for me to have so little to do to organise an event. I just had to help them promote it and remember to turn up on the night to make my speech. For them to be so hands-on made me think it was more than just Laura being in the right place at the right time. It was like they were destined to meet! The night raised over £4,000, which was absolutely incredible.

I was stunned when he told me about his plans to organise a fundraising quiz in the Taunton area as well. He felt that it would make sense to have an event that people from the local area could attend as well, and who was I to disagree? I had to do more of the organisation this time but seeing as it was local it wasn't too hard, and a very supportive pub landlord agreed to host the night for free, going out of his way to promote it as well. Just the fact that Paul was going to be there meant that the tickets sold out almost faster than they could be printed, and we raised over £2,000. It was nearly a little less, though, as we caught one lovely lady with her hand in the charity pot that held our takings for the night.

"Well you shouldn't leave it unattended, should you?" she shrugged.

What can you say to that really? We were utterly speechless. She'd been earmarked as a troublemaker all night; she had originally turned up without a ticket and hadn't told us that it was inside with the rest of her team, instead flying into a rage and demanding to be let in. When we found out the situation we relented, but the whole of her team became a real nuisance all night, and it almost ruined the atmosphere. One of the guys complained that we'd run out of raffle tickets but we sold over 1,000 of them that night and kept announcing that they were available, trying to make sure everyone knew when they were running low. He even had a go at Paul, and this was what bothered me most. Paul had really gone out of his way to support us. I couldn't believe it when the guy found me later on after I'd made a speech about the cause and carried on complaining.

"I'll be sending you an e-mail to make my complaint official," he said.

"Thank you, sir," I replied. "I will look forward to receiving it."

What else could I do? I've found that people like him are always the same; if you give them any further information, they will use it against you and can be quite manipulative in doing so, making you look like the bad guy. If I just humoured him, then there would be nothing more he could do. The e-mail never came, presumably because he'd found something else to complain about and forgotten about me. It was obvious he just wanted to upset me, and I have no idea why. It has never made sense to me why some adults feel the need to behave like this. Everyone else had been pleasant and enjoyed the evening, but this one group seemed determined to spoil it for everyone. I just hoped it hadn't put Paul off, but then he'd probably dealt with plenty of hecklers before at his comedy shows, and he didn't seem especially put out. In fact, he told me he'd be back next year to do it all again.

I must say I was relieved, but I just couldn't get the disruptive team out of my head. I was used to dealing with the odd unpleasant person but what had happened did play on my mind. There was just no need to be like that; it was cruel. What made it most bizarre was that they must have been in their late 50s but were behaving like stroppy teenagers. I guess some people never grow up.

When I had seen how much Paul was willing to help I thought maybe others would do the same, and I had one person in particular on my radar. I had been reluctant to approach him so far because he was Ben's nephew. I felt like I would be putting him in an awkward position and it would be difficult for him to say no. In the end, though, I decided to drop him an e-mail, making sure he knew that he was under no obligation to say yes to anything.

His name was Harley, and he was one half of a popular music duo called Rizzle Kicks. They'd had a few hit singles and so they were familiar to most people even in sleepy old Somerset. I thought it would be fantastic to have their support, but as soon as I sent the e-mail I began feeling awkward, picturing him opening it and not really knowing how to respond. Luckily, he put me out of my misery almost straight away and made my day by telling me he would be more than happy to help because I was family. I was very touched that he considered me to be so and was excited about the ways we could work together.

I e-mailed him back soon afterwards to suggest some possibilities. I received no reply this time, but we were all going on a family holiday together in the near future, so I was hoping we could discuss it then. Ben told me not to mention it as we were going on holiday and so it wasn't the time or the place to talk about work, but we were picking him up from the airport and it seemed natural that it might come up in conversation. I wanted to ask him the minute he got into the back seat of the car, but I managed to bite my tongue.

"Sorry I hadn't replied to your e-mail yet, Adam," said Harley, after we'd been chatting for about a minute. "I just thought it would be better to wait until now so we can talk properly, face-to-face."

Well, it would have been rude to say no, wouldn't it? For most of the journey to the hotel, we talked shop, which I don't think impressed Ben very much, but I was absolutely euphoric. He had basically said yes to everything, and that he and his bandmate Jordan would be delighted to be ambassadors of Stand Against Violence. For the rest of the week, we just spent some time together as a family without mentioning the charity, and I have to admit it was lovely to have some time off.

We stayed in touch when we got back and Harley put me in touch with his manager. After my experience with Paul's manager I was all geared up for a great discussion, but instead I received an e-mail telling me that the guys already supported two other charities and were extremely busy, so what they could offer me would be limited. Harley hadn't seemed to think he would be too busy, so I found this hard to understand. I wondered if his manager had been affronted that I had gone straight to Harley and not through him but seeing as he was family this seemed strange. The manager did say he would help in any way he could, but he said no to pretty much everything I requested and stopped replying to my e-mails. I didn't want to make things awkward by asking Harley to have a word, and so I backed off for a while. The more I thought about it, though, the more I felt like I was letting another great opportunity slip by. I arranged a face-to-face meeting so we could talk about everything properly and I could find out what he would help with and what he wouldn't. I thought maybe if we met we would get on and would understand better where each other were coming from.

We had been really keen for Rizzle Kicks to perform in Taunton as part of an event to mark the 10th anniversary of Lloyd's death, which would be a celebration of his life.

"I don't think that's a good idea," he said. "They're not famous enough to attract a big crowd in a place like that. It would be a flop."

This seemed very odd to me, as on the other hand he was telling me how busy they were, so they were obviously in demand. He did agree to a social media competition and some signed CDs, so he didn't flat out refuse to help, but I knew if it had been up to Harley we would have been able to do so much more together, which was frustrating.

There was an event in London that seemed to fit with the manager's idea of what was okay, so I approached him and he agreed, telling me that we would speak soon to sort out the details. I let the venue know that he had said yes in principle, but I was waiting to hear more. Two months went by and they were anxious to get Rizzle Kicks confirmed for their event. I went back to the manager but there was still nothing, and the venue were understandably concerned, so I forwarded an e-mail they had sent me with an abrupt request for him to let us know what was happening. This time I heard back pretty quickly, and I could tell straight away that he was not happy.

"You've got a nerve," he said. "Slagging me off to the venue? Well, you can be certain that Rizzle Kicks will not be appearing at the event, and from this point onwards I will withdraw all support from Stand Against Violence."

I looked through the thread of e-mails and further down the page was one in which I had said something along the lines of "I've not heard from him for a while but I often don't when he doesn't really want to do something."

At first, I thought, "What have I done?" and was pretty upset with myself. By forwarding one e-mail I'd ruined the opportunity, but I started to reason and remembered that nothing I said was untrue. I didn't mean to slag him off, I was just trying to explain to the venue why the band weren't confirmed. Maybe I should have just given up on the idea when the manager made it clear early on he wasn't willing to support us, but because Harley had been so keen I held onto the hope that we could arrange something. Maybe I should have gone back to Harley and asked him to try and smooth things over, but I didn't want to put him in a difficult position. I hadn't intended for the manager to see that e-mail, but I thought if his support had been genuine he'd have wanted to reassure me that he did want to help and was sorry I felt that way. I appreciate that he was busy but a quick acknowledgment e-mail to tell me this would only have taken a minute and would have saved a lot of time for everyone. It seemed that he was looking for an excuse from the start to withdraw support, and perhaps it was best for everyone to move on. It seemed my instinct had been right that I might make things awkward for Harley by asking him for support. When Paul came on board it was through his request to help and his manager was only too happy to support him in this. Unfortunately, this seems rare.

It wasn't long before a new collaborator was introduced to me. He was one of the last people I would have expected to work with, and he may not have had the same reach as a celebrity supporter, but his input would arguably have an even greater impact.

Meeting a Murderer

"I've got a letter for you if you want it," he said. "I wrote it to sum up everything I want you to know."

I took the letter and reached over to shake the hand of the man who had set all of this in motion. Ten years had passed since the night Lloyd died. Ten years is a long time. The same amount of time before Lloyd died I'd cleaned him up when he projectile vomited all over himself as an 8-year-old boy. He would have been a man in his late twenties if he'd been alive the day I met Jay for the first time, and he might even have had an 8-year-old boy of his own. I expect he'd have wished Uncle Adam had been there to clean up if there had been a similar vomiting incident! Because of the actions of the man I'd just met, Lloyd had lost his life when he was just about to turn 18. This seemed very odd to me. The man who stood in front of me now bore little resemblance to the teenage lad I remembered from the trial. He looked like somebody I could imagine being friends with, and from the time I'd spent with him that day I couldn't imagine him being violent. To imagine him as a killer just seemed absurd.

My parents were less keen than I was, which I understood, but they never tried to stand in my way, and the day seemed to come round in no time. Before I knew it I was on the train to Newmarket, where the meeting would be taking place the following day. It wasn't until I got to the hotel and tried to speak to my dad on the phone that the enormity of what I was doing hit home. I had been on the phone to my dad when I first found out that Lloyd had died. Just for a moment, it was as if no time had passed between then and now. What was I doing? I was about to be face-to-face with one of the men who had been responsible. So much buried emotion from the decade in between burst to the surface. I hung up the phone straight away because I just couldn't get my words out.

My dad tried to call back straight away, thinking we'd been cut off. It took me a while to answer, and I still found it hard to speak when I did. He twigged what was happening, and I poured out all of my fears.

"I just don't know how I'll react when I see him, Dad," I sobbed. "I might burst into tears like I have now. I might shout at him. I might just take one look at him, turn around and walk straight out. I don't want to do any of those things but Lloyd's dead because of him and his friends. I don't know if I'll be able to stay calm."

"Just remember why you're doing this," my dad told me. "Mum says she'll pick you up afterwards if you don't feel like getting the train back."

"Oh, no, she doesn't have to drive all that way," I said straight away, and my composure returned.

We kept talking, and I poured everything out. I did feel better for having spoken to my parents, but it took me a long time to get to sleep. It would have helped if I could have had a glass of wine or two but the bar at the hotel was shut. I was sent some lovely messages on Facebook from friends, which cheered me up a little bit, but it was one of the longest nights of my life.

Meeting Jay was something I'd felt compelled to do for quite a while. At the time of the trial, I felt like his two co-defendants showed no remorse, but he had at least seemed to realise the consequences of his actions and I believed he may be sorry for what he had caused. One night his face appeared briefly in a dream, and from that point onwards there was an idea I just couldn't get out of my head. A number of years had now passed, and maybe it would soon be time for him to be released from prison. If he was genuinely remorseful for what he had done then what better way would there be of getting our message across than to have Jay work alongside us in some way? In a way, I thought I must be crazy to even consider that, but then if he had rehabilitated and I tried to hold him back then what had the work I'd been doing all these years really been about? If he had a chance to come out of prison and live a more meaningful life then of course that was something I would support. If he came out and was given no opportunities then slid back into his old ways, what would have been achieved through his time in prison?

These thoughts kept me awake at night, and I wondered what my parents would think. Could I really expect them to see me stand side by side with one of the guys who killed their son? This was a real concern, but the more I thought about it the more I knew I wanted the chance to talk to him. Just when I was becoming borderline obsessed with the idea I had a call from Alex, our probation liaison officer.

"I wanted you to know that Jay's probation hearing is approaching, and he may be moved to an open prison," she began after we had caught up a little bit. "As part of this we need a victim support statement from you all, and you'll have to let me know any restrictions you'd want to impose."

"Okay," I replied. "Now, this may come as a surprise but what would be the possibility of me actually meeting him?"

"Well, it actually does happen more often than you would realise," she said straight away. "And more to the point, this is something Jay has offered. If you really wanted to meet him I could mediate between you. It's thought to be very beneficial for rehabilitation."

I paused for breath. If I hadn't asked about meeting Jay the chance would have been offered to me anyway. I couldn't refuse now.

"Do you think he truly has changed?" I asked.

"I'm afraid I would need his permission to release any information," she admitted. "And in theory, he could refuse."

"If he does refuse that tells me all I need to know," I said. "If he accepts then we can take it from there."

I did have a few doubts. Was he still a potential danger, and if I helped him to be released would history repeat itself? What would my parents think? Would I really want to meet him when it came to it? I had purposefully tried not to think too much about Lloyd's killers over the years, but now this one guy in particular I felt I had to at least talk to. How much more meaningful would our workshops be if young people could hear his side of the story as well, and the impact it had on his life? A number of lives were changed that day, including his. He may still have a life, which Lloyd did not because of his actions, but what kind of a life was it? At the age when many young people would be starting a career, going to University, meeting partners, and enjoying their youth, he had gone to prison. What kind of life would he have when he came out? Would anyone employ a convicted murderer? A split-second decision he made when he was just a teenager and look where it got him. What could be a better message for young people to not make the same mistakes?

Of course I could be getting way ahead of myself. Would he even want to get involved? Did he genuinely regret what he had done? I finally summoned the courage to ask my parents what they thought, and they were surprisingly calm.

"If it would help you to talk to him then you should do it," my dad told me. Neither he nor my mum wanted to meet Jay, which I understood, but I contacted Alex almost straight away to try and put things in motion.

She had spoken to Jay, who also wanted to arrange a meeting. He explained that he didn't want to cause us any more pain than he already had, and so he would not be moving to Somerset when he was released, but if any of us wanted to meet with him he would answer any questions we had, if that would help us in any way. I had no way of knowing if he was genuine or if he was just trying to influence the parole board, but I had to give him the benefit of the doubt, especially as he was the one I'd seen hints of remorse from back in court.

I spoke frequently with Alex leading up to the meeting, to try and prepare myself. The reality was that I had no idea how I would react when I saw Jay, just like at the trial. This was entirely different, as it would just be me and him in the room along with Alex and perhaps a prison officer. At the trial were the judge, lawyers, my family, the defendants' families, the jury, the press . . . how I would respond when I met him face-to-face could not be compared. As the day drew nearer I tried to put it out of my mind, but on the journey up I had several spasms of anxiety.

The idea to meet with Jay was another thing that had come to me out of the blue, as if Lloyd had put it there. Before I went to sleep that night I said to him "It's your fault I'm here, so you'd better bloody be there too!"

The next morning I had expected to wake up feeling just as anxious as I had the night before, but now the day had arrived I actually felt quite calm. Now I would be able to get it over with, and later that day I would be going back home. There was nothing more to be afraid of.

Alex was going to drive me to the prison. It was a 30-minute journey to HMP Highpoint, where I would meet Jay, and it gave us plenty of time to talk. I bombarded her with questions, trying to feel as prepared as possible for the meeting. I had written some questions for Jay in the hope that there would be no awkward silences from me, but strangely Alex got far more of an interrogation than he would!

"I think Jay's nervous about the meeting too," she told me. "There's nothing for you to worry about. Remember he didn't have to do this: he agreed to it because he wants you to know what happened."

I was expecting there to be locks and bars everywhere, but this was not the case. HMP Highpoint is a category C prison, which means it isn't maximum security. There are a number of courses available for the inmates, and some are able to leave the prison for work placements during the day, all with an aim towards them finding employment upon release and being less likely to continue pursuing crime. This might make it seem like Jay received no punishment in prison, but he wasn't in HMP Highpoint for much of his sentence. I have to admit, my feelings on prison as a punishment versus a chance for rehabilitation are complex. First of all, I do believe that prison should be a punishment. The fact is that what Jay did resulted in my brother's death, which tore my life apart, tore my family's lives apart, and had a profound impact on a number of other lives: his own family, Lloyd's friends, the paramedics who tried to save his life . . . way more lives than you would imagine.

All of this happened because of one wrong decision. Did he mean for Lloyd to die? No, I honestly don't believe he did. Was his life torn apart as well? Yes, it was. Spending years in prison away from his family when he was so young was a punishment. But what about all of the opportunities he had for learning? Well, what would be the point in prison if he had no chance of changing his life when he was released? He would almost inevitably go back to the same lifestyle through a lack of alternatives and would end up back inside time and time again. Some would argue that he deserved no chance of life because his actions had robbed Lloyd of just that, but before I met him I could already see that this would mean more damage had been caused by his actions than was necessary.

I could tell we were in a prison, but apart from the standard security check when we went in we moved through pretty quickly, and before I knew it we were in a corridor leading to the prison chapel, where the meeting would be taking place. I hadn't seen Jay, even a photo of him, since the trial. To be completely honest I was expecting an almost 30-year-old Burberry clad overgrown teenager to be waiting for me. He was already in the room and after Alex asked if I was ready she opened the door, and the moment had arrived.

I made the briefest eye contact when I walked in and Jay's expression gave nothing away. My first impression took me by surprise. He was wearing a shirt and jeans and looked nothing like I remembered him. I had real trouble associating him with what he had done. It was almost as if Jay had been unable to make the meeting and they'd sent an actor in his place, hoping I wouldn't notice.

"Okay, Adam I want you to meet Jay. Jay, this is Adam," said Alex, who would facilitate the conversation.

I knew that Jay was nervous, and I was too, so I tried to just treat it like any other meeting. I referred to my list of questions.

"Jay, I was wondering if you could take me through what happened that night?" I asked.

Jay did exactly that. He told me the story of what happened as if he was telling any other anecdote, except his expression remained neutral throughout. He left nothing out.

"I remember there had been a disagreement between one of my co-defendants and another of our friends," he told me. "So the atmosphere had already changed from the celebratory mood earlier on when I'd scored the winning goal in a football match. After that I was rejected by a girl and my friends gave me a lot of stick for it . . . then I got in a playfight with one of my friends when we left the pub. It quickly turned into a real fight. My friend got the better of it and I said I'd had enough, but my pride was hurt, and that was when I decided the next person I saw I would start a fight with."

I couldn't take it in. This guy was telling me that Lloyd had died because of wounded pride? I felt angry, but I kept everything to myself for now because there was a lot more I wanted to know. People get their pride wounded every day and nobody dies because of it. There had to be more to it than that.

Over the remainder of our time together Jay told me a simplified version of the chapters you read earlier on. As I listened two things hit home. The first was that his actions had definitely led to Lloyd's death. The second was that the man who sat in front of me now was different to the teenage lad who had made that mistake. It was clear that he was never proud of what he did. He hadn't spent his time in prison trading off his reputation as a killer and planning how he was going to boss the streets upon his release. This was a young man who had really considered the impact of his actions and had made an effort to change his ways. When I saw his foot I had real difficulty picturing it stamping on my brother's head. At the time of Jay's sentence, I thought it was too short, but it was clear that prison had been about rehabilitation for him, and I believed that he was genuinely remorseful.

Despite the end result of the conversation, I was hearing details for the first time about the attack that led to Lloyd's death. It had a different impact on me to the reconstruction we had filmed in that I was actually hearing first-hand from one of his attackers what had happened. Jay was telling me things he had never said in court, and my overactive imagination was playing out the whole gruesome scene. I couldn't help welling up, but I didn't explode with sobs like I had outside the courtroom. I thought back to that time.

"Jay, I noticed that you were trembling in the courtroom when you were sentenced. Do you remember why that was?"

"Because I was scared," he sighed. "I was terrified of going to prison, and I would have done anything to get out of that situation. I guess it was just the total loss of control. I was about to be locked up for years and there was nothing I could do to stop it."

"Was it to do with remorse in any way?" I asked.

"Honestly," he said after a brief pause, "at the time . . . no. I was just scared. That was all I was thinking of. The remorse came later because it took a while before I could actually admit my actions had led to Lloyd's death. Now I can say that if it wasn't for my actions he would probably still be alive. It's entirely my fault that Lloyd lost his life."

As we continued to talk I focused a bit less on what he was saying and a bit more on his overall manner. I doubt he was scared of me attacking him, but it did take a lot of courage to be so honest and open about being to blame for my brother losing his life. He answered all of my questions, and I could somehow just tell he was being truthful. He hadn't tried to make himself look innocent, and calmly told me what happened, without trying to justify himself. It was the strangest feeling, but as the conversation moved on I felt like he was pleasant to talk to. It must be so hard for people to understand, but I just think of Jay as somebody I know. I've only met him twice, but I feel no hatred towards him for what he did. He's such a different person nowadays.

"What do you think you'll be doing when you get out of here?" I said.

"Well, I'd like to have a partner and a family, but to tell you the truth I don't feel like I deserve it. I'm not sure what career prospects I'll have, but again I've only got myself to blame for that. I actually messed up quite a good opportunity before all of this. If I hadn't then maybe I'd just have been focused on that. Maybe I'd never have gone out that night. If I could change that I would, but that's the one thing I can never change."

"Do you think there's anything that could have stopped you from doing what you did to Lloyd?"

"On the actual night, I don't think there would have been," he said. "I was a ticking time bomb, and I would have got in a fight with someone that night, no matter who it was. Maybe if I'd gone to prison before then it would have changed me, but I'd never been in a proper fight before, and I'd only done a bit of petty crime. Anti-social behaviour, theft, that kind of thing."

"So do you think the justice system's too soft on young offenders? Is it actually failing them?"

"Yes it is," he replied, without even pausing for thought.

This had been my opinion for a long time, and to have it confirmed by someone who had actually been through the system was fascinating. I didn't hear many details about Jay's past the first time I met him, but I did hear of how he had a troubled upbringing and had a lot of anger as a result. I know the group he became involved with were known around Taunton for violence and anti-social behaviour, but whatever punishments they had received were clearly having no effect, as they just carried on behaving in the same way. I don't believe that young people like these are just bad through and through. We are often products of our circumstances, and if we don't find a good direction in life it's easy to fall in with the wrong crowd. The wrong crowd is often made up of a group of people who are all lacking in direction or had problems at home and so gravitated towards people at school who were in the same boat. Then their shared anger led to an escalation of aggressive behaviour. Without proper guidance, it's easy to go down the wrong path in life, and this is why we need to do more as a society to properly engage with young people.

When our time was over we all got up and I shook Jay's hand, which was when he gave me the letter.

"I believe that everyone deserves a second chance, Jay," I told him. "Don't doubt what you can achieve when you're released. I believe, after talking to you today, that you're genuine in your remorse. You deserve to get your life back on track."

He looked at me with what seemed like confusion, but I guess it was the last thing he was expecting to hear from me. I mentioned that if he wanted to get involved in some violence prevention work with us we would be open to that, and we left it that we would keep communicating through Alex. I'm not sure what you might be feeling to have read this, but I truly do believe that Jay deserves a second chance. I wouldn't say I forgive him, and I don't feel like I need to tell him that in order to move on, but I hope that anyone who reads this will feel the same way I do. He made a terrible mistake when he was young, which led to someone losing their life. That person was my brother. His actions caused extreme pain to me and my family, which we still feel even now, even if it's not as intense as it was at the time. He knows that.

I believe that Jay used his time in prison well. He reflected on his actions, he felt genuine remorse and he tried to ensure he took the steps necessary to prevent it from happening again. I genuinely wish him well in life. If he had not shown remorse then I'm not sure I would, but when I talked to him that day I felt his remorse, and I believed that he has changed. He was in prison for 12 years. That's 12 years of his life he'll never get back. We will never know how many years of Lloyd's life he took away, but to say he deserves no life would mean it wasn't just Lloyd's life that was lost that day. If he goes back to his old ways out of prison the lives of his mum, his brothers, and anyone else who happens to get on the wrong side of him will also be ruined, as well as his own life. It doesn't have to be that way, and why would I want it to be? How much of a hypocrite would I be if I wanted to ruin the rest of Jay's life when the charity I'd set up had been all about preventing lives from being ruined?

"How do you feel now?" asked Alex when we were back in the car.

"I'm glad I went through with it," I admitted. "Some of it was very uncomfortable to listen to, but it was the truth, and I'm glad I've got a better picture of what happened."

So it was all over. All the anxiety and upset of the night before, and in the end, I felt completely justified in wanting to make the meeting happen. Sadly, neither of Jay's co-defendants seem to have shown any remorse to date. A couple of years after I met Jay for the first time I heard that Andrew was due for release, but he expressed no desire to meet me and I wasn't especially keen to meet him, because he was still maintaining that he couldn't remember attacking Lloyd. I have always had real trouble understanding this. If someone can get so drunk that they can't remember killing someone then why would they drink in the first place? If they knew they lost control that much then wouldn't they be equally worried that they might be putting themselves in danger as well as others? Seeing as he smirked when he received the sentence and swaggered out of court like he'd won a gold medal it seemed like prison was a badge of honour for him, and from what I've heard since it doesn't seem as if he changed his mind for the whole 13 years he was locked up. I find this hard to understand, but before I met Jay I was half expecting him to be the same. Maybe some people just don't want to change. Only time will tell.

Andrew is now out of prison but isn't living in the same area as me or any of my family. I'm unlikely to bump into him, and if I did, I'm not sure I would recognise him, considering how different Jay looked from the days of the trial. Obviously, I really hope he doesn't get involved in any more violence, but I have my concerns that he has the same mindset as when he first went to prison. Nothing I've heard has suggested otherwise. Their other co-defendant was involved in some more instances of violence over the years, but never any that led to further loss of life. I find it hard to wrap my head round the way that someone could continue to pursue a life of violence after he'd seen someone die because of it, and two of his friends get lengthy prison sentences. I'm not sure what was going on in his life to make it so difficult to escape the cycle of violence. Maybe one day I will find out, maybe not, but because Jay has changed maybe it will make all the difference in the world to someone's family. I guess it has to his own.

Jay: Six

When I met Adam for the first time it was tough. No matter what progress I'd made at Grendon, I was coming face-to-face for the first time with the man whose brother had died because of me. I'm not sure what I was expecting, but I felt nervous about talking to him. I decided before we met that I would just tell him the truth. He deserved that. I wanted him to know how sorry I was, but I would have understood if that meant nothing to him. When he told me at the end of our meeting that he wanted me to have a second chance in life I was taken aback. I just thought what an amazing person Adam was to be able to say that to me and mean it. He hadn't forgiven me, and I wouldn't expect him to, but he realised that what happened to Lloyd was a tragic mistake, and I hadn't meant for anyone to die. Ten years had passed now since it happened, and I'm not the same person I was then. He saw that, and he knew that I couldn't change what happened, but he didn't want it to define the rest of my life. He wanted me to try and have a life going forward. For that, I can never express how grateful I am.

I was released from prison in 2017. I'm very lucky to have met a wonderful partner, and I've even become a dad. I work as a personal trainer. I have a good life, and whether I deserve that or not is debatable, but it would be selfish of me to think I don't and to act like I don't because it would have a negative impact on my kids. It would be a massive insult to my mum, to Adam, to myself, and to a number of people really if I threw away this amazing second chance I've been given. I don't have to try that hard to be a different person, because it's just who I am nowadays, but there are still certain situations that make me aware of my responses.

I'm very aware of my surroundings now. Of course I still get angry because that's life and everyone does from time to time. Everyone has emotions. I'm very aware, though, of who I want to be as a person, and you'll never find me drinking with a bunch of lads in a pub these days. Not because I think if I did I would have a fight again, but because I'm a different person and drinking with a bunch of lads isn't what I enjoy doing nowadays. Back then I would have seen a certain excitement in a situation where it could all kick off, and I might even have gone looking for it, but that's definitely not who I am now. Looking back I suppose there was always potential that I could have found myself in the situation I did. Not necessarily one caused by me, but by any one of the group we were in.

My idea of loyalties and what life is all about are very different. When I was growing up I had a deep hatred for my mum's husband at the time, and I don't have that anymore, but of course I still have anger. If I was to see him it would almost certainly stir those feelings up, but I'm a lot more self-aware now and I'm more aware than most of what the consequences of venting your anger can be. By facing up to what I've caused I've been able to become the person I am today. I would once have had thoughts of seeking revenge on my mum's husband, but I've let go of that now.

Because I have a good life now, I feel more guilty than ever, but I try not to dwell on it. I can't; I don't just have myself to think about. Having said that, I really am so sorry for what happened, and I hope Adam knows that. I'd be lying if I said I think about what I did every day. I think the main reason is that I just couldn't possibly think about the seriousness of what I caused every day, because I wouldn't be able to function in life. I'm not in denial anymore, but I just can't spend too long thinking about what I did without it having an effect on how I can get through the day. It's really deep to think about what I did, that my actions led to somebody's death. As unfair as it might seem, considering how Adam and his family will never forget, I just have to try and put it out of my head sometimes.

When I'm at the gym now and some lads ask me if I wanna go out for a few drinks I always say no, because I can't put myself in that situation again. Sometimes when there's a guy in the gym who's showing a bit of attitude I have to take a step back and think about what could happen as a result of me losing my cool. It's always in the back of my head, but not always in the front now, as it was when I was in prison. I'm very aware of the need to walk away, to not get involved in a confrontation.

A lot of the guys I used to hang out with have added me on Facebook and said hello, but I keep my circle small, and I haven't tried to seek out new or old friends. My brother lives nearby and I've got my girlfriend of course, so that's pretty much my immediate circle now.

I did go and visit my mum in Somerset a while back, but I had no desire to see anyone else. I associate them with who I used to be, and that's not who I am now. I've got a new life. Things have moved on a lot in twelve years, and to think I would come out of prison and go back to doing the same things I was doing before just seems ridiculous. I barely even drink nowadays. I might have the odd glass of wine at home in the evening but that's it. Exercise is how I deal with everything. If I'm feeling particularly stressed any time I'll just go for a run or have a workout at the gym. That really helps to take the edge off things, and then I'm ready to deal with whatever else I have to in the day.

Looking forward, I think this is my life now. I'm lucky enough to have a family of my own, and I want my kids to have a secure upbringing. I've got security now with my family and my job, so there's no reason for me to go back to my old ways. I know I don't ever want to go to prison again, but I don't want to be doing any of the things that might send me back there.

If anyone can learn anything from my story, it would be simple. Don't get in a fight. People are more fragile than you might think, and that could apply to you or to whoever you get in a fight with. I had no concept of the fact that Lloyd might have lost his life, even the morning after the fight. I may have been in denial, but I knew what the group I hung out with were like, and it never even entered my head that one of them might kill someone. All it took was one wrong decision and then there were years of pain and suffering for a number of people, and no future for a young guy who was just about to turn 18. That's what I caused. I didn't mean to, but I did. A few young lads venting their anger was all it took. If that doesn't frighten you it should. If you think it wouldn't happen to you, it could. Maybe I am lucky to have the life I do now, but I only have it because I changed. If I went back to my old ways I would lose everything I've been blessed with in an instant.

When Adam asked me to be involved with this book I wanted to help, because if someone like the teenager I was could hear my story and realise what could happen if they carried on that way then maybe it would stop someone like Lloyd from losing his life needlessly. What happened to him, because of me, was such a waste. There's no way of knowing for sure what would have happened if I hadn't started a fight, or if I hadn't called my friends back, but I feel pretty certain Lloyd would still be alive today if I'd just carried on walking and let my anger go. I hated my mum's husband for what he did to her, and how scared he made her feel, but instead of trying to be better than that I took my anger towards him out on someone who didn't deserve it. He might have set the events in motion that led to my anger, but he didn't start the fight that led to Lloyd's death. I did. We all have choices. I don't want anyone to make that same mistake.

I wasn't an angry kid from the beginning, I never wanted to hurt people, I just wanted to play football and hang out with my friends. I had a difficult time growing up, but that wasn't the reason for what happened. I knew right from wrong, but I messed up some things in my life and it left me without much of a direction. I was angry, and I didn't think about the consequences if I let it out. Your actions have consequences. Many people learn lessons the hard way, but this is one lesson you don't want to have to learn. I will always know deep down that someone lost their life because of me, and I will always know that it could have been avoided if I'd made a better decision. This is the message I would try to put across time and time again. There are consequences to violence. Don't let it be you who finds out the hard way.

Snakes and Ladders

So my story is full of ups and downs. That much will be obvious by now. Some of the best things that have happened for the charity I have to pinch myself when I think of. We have also had some unimaginably bad fortune that might have made me give up on the whole thing if it hadn't been for the high points to balance them out. Really it's been like a game of snakes and ladders, which I suppose could be an analogy for life itself.

I've not really talked about the impact Lloyd's death had on his friends all that much, but I know those who were there when he was attacked were profoundly affected. How could they not be? Some developed insomnia, some drifted apart from each other because what they experienced together was just too harrowing to talk about, I know some were deeply traumatised. A number of them have also been more than willing to lend their support to Stand Against Violence, which I hope has been cathartic for them in some way, as it has been for me. Sadly one instance of this took an unexpected and highly disappointing turn, which I am still struggling to understand.

One of Lloyd's good friends, who was in close proximity to him when he was attacked, became one of our key volunteers. He went out of his way to help us and we were overjoyed with his dedication and enthusiasm. There came a time, though, when something didn't seem quite right, and he ended up cheating us out of a fairly substantial sum of money. He used our name to get people to buy tickets for events, but then we saw none of the money. I wanted to believe that there was some kind of explanation, but it soon became obvious there was not. What began as a fantastic partnership ended in a bitter court case, and I've never understood how it happened. He must have had his reasons, but I guess only he will ever truly know. I don't know how he thought he would get away with what he did, which suggests that he was maybe acting out of desperation and needed the money. This doesn't excuse his behaviour, but it would be an explanation. I hope whatever difficulty or personal issue led to this deception is now in the past.

We also had a difficult experience with the filmmaker we worked with. He didn't deliver what he had promised when it came to the 3D film, which almost made the launch event a disaster. We had invested money in his time, but he hadn't taken it seriously enough. I said as long as he paid the money back there would be no issue, but he no longer had any of it. I asked the board what they thought I should do and there was a unanimous decision that I had no real option but to take him to court, to try and figure out a repayment plan. We ended up seeing none of the money again, and as a charity who have struggled to obtain funding at times, it was very hard to take.

I wish those guys had talked to me, or someone else, about whatever difficulties they were having before taking such extreme measures. It was especially sad because we had worked so well with both of them in the past. It has made me more cautious about who I trust, and I have been torn between the approaches of making people earn my trust from the beginning or giving people the benefit of the doubt but being constantly on my guard. Taking risks is vital in order for progression to be possible, but when my trust was abused and it proved costly it did make me more risk-averse, which was not how I wanted to be.

I did throw caution to the wind by taking some fundraising matters into my own hands and agreeing to a skydive. I had said a definite no to this at first, but then I thought about an abseil I had taken part in the year before. The only other abseil I had done was at school aged 13, and it made me shed tears of terror! As you can imagine, this gave plenty of ammunition to my classmates and I decided to never put myself through the same humiliation again. That was until one of our volunteers organised a fundraising abseil and some friends and family were getting involved. I decided I would join them. What was the worst that could happen?

Nobody put any pressure on me to join in, but I decided it was time to face my fears. I was actually feeling pretty calm until it was my turn to go over the edge. In an instant, all of my previous terrors came flooding back, but somehow I managed to go through with it, and without crying. However, I did grip the rope so hard that my fingers had gone into some kind of spasm and had to be almost prised off. I might still be there now if I hadn't been able to remove them from the rope.

The main thing was that I had survived the abseil. I can't say I enjoyed it, but how much worse could a skydive be? Okay, so it was quite a few thousand feet higher up, and I wouldn't be attached to a rope . . . oh! I tried to get it out of my head, but when the day came round I was glad that our jump was scheduled for the morning, so we would get it out of the way. Yeah, right! I had been told beforehand that you don't jump if there are too many clouds around, for safety reasons, and we arrived at 9am to skies so overcast it was like the end of the world was imminent. Oh, well, that's that, then. Shame we couldn't do it. Let's go home . . . no! We would just wait until the clouds had parted. 10am came around, then 11, then midday. Still, nothing had changed. It was very different to the wait for the jury's verdict during Lloyd's trial, but it was a similarly long day. When would we get to jump? Would it even happen today? Would they make us do it another day if not?

Mid-afternoon arrived and the clouds were still taunting us. I may have been nervous about the jump, but I hadn't spent all that time preparing for the day just for such an anti-climax. I looked around at everyone else who had joined the team and was once again overwhelmed by the amount of support. Some were friends of mine, but all were willing to throw themselves out of a plane to help me, and how many can say they have people who are willing to do that for them? We had to do this. As evening rolled around the clouds rolled away, and it was finally time to go. Now my nerves came back with a vengeance. I was very anxious about losing my tummy when falling through the air, and I mentioned this to my instructor, who would be attached to me by a harness.

"Honestly, mate, that doesn't happen," he reassured me. "It doesn't even seem that high when you're up there because everything's so small."

"Okay," I said, but his expression told me he could tell I felt anything but.

"You'll be alright, I mean it," he smiled. "I bet you'll want to do it all again afterwards."

"I'm not sure about that," I laughed.

At 7pm we finally had our chance. When the plane took off I knew there was no turning back, and I shut my eyes for a moment, wondering what on earth I had let myself in for. I mean seriously, I didn't have to do this. What was I thinking? Suddenly I couldn't stop a smile from breaking out.

"You'd have absolutely loved this, wouldn't you? Nutter!" I said to Lloyd in my head. It has to be said, a number of activities I've done for the charity would have been far more Lloyd's thing than mine, and in a way he's been able to live through me. Leaping out of a plane would have been something he'd have literally jumped at the chance to do. Is that where the expression comes from?

His presence with me grew as I looked out of the window and saw that my instructor had been right. The buildings and fields I could see way below looked just like a farm playset Lloyd and I had when we were very small. Somehow I just knew that everything would be okay.

This was it. The door opened and there was nothing left to do but jump out. It all happened in what felt like seconds. I felt no fear as I fell, my tummy stayed calm, all I remember was the noise. I could barely hear myself think as we plummeted, but before I knew what was happening the cord of my parachute was pulled and the harness yanked upwards, digging into my armpits with a force that left me bruised for a week. When the pain subsided I tried to get my bearings. There was a stillness and a silence

I had never experienced. I was falling from a great height but I barely seemed to be moving at all, and it was so quiet I could literally hear my own thoughts. Everything just looked incredible from up here. I was seeing the world from a totally different perspective to usual, as if I had the real view version of Google Maps implanted into my brain!

"Don't forget to look up," shouted my instructor. I looked up and straight away I saw why he had said it. Banks of fluffy clouds in the distance rolled lazily towards the setting sun, which gave them a warm orange glow. I'd never seen anything so beautiful, and the tears came straight away. I was partly sad that Lloyd never got to experience this, but I also couldn't remember the last time I felt so peaceful. I guess they call it mindfulness; all I was focused on was the present moment, and I was filled with the kind of serenity I long for in life but never quite seem to find. I wasn't really thinking about much at all once I settled into the experience. I was just hanging in the air, floating down towards the earth like a balloon. It was so lovely, and it was over far too soon. I have never since experienced the same level of tranquillity, and it feels just typical of me that I have to jump out of a plane to get the same feeling others might from reading a good book, going to a spa, or lounging in a field on a sunny day. Everything the instructor had said to me earlier came back, and I can definitely see why people get hooked.

I felt it was important when it came to the abseil and the skydive to put my money where my mouth was, but our most successful fundraising endeavour yet was mostly the work of one of our trustees along with a local lady I knew who was involved with a PR company. After watching an episode of *Russell Howard's Good News* the trustee got in touch with the PR lady and suggested the idea; nothing ventured, nothing gained. She had a contact for Russell and to our great fortune, he was up for coming to perform. To cut a long story short, it was an absolutely remarkable evening. Russell and a few other comics from the circuit had an absolutely packed Wellsprings Leisure Centre laughing non-stop. It was just pure euphoria from start to finish and the evening raised over £20,000 for us including a raffle. Obviously, this was a fantastic result, and we were all grinning like

Cheshire cats for days.

I got to meet Russell after the show, and he doesn't look especially tall on TV but he was about the same as me—5'9", and this wasn't the only way we seemed to be on a level.

"Thank you so much for this, Russell," I beamed. "It's amazing how successful this has been for us. Maybe we could do it again sometime?"

"Yeah, for sure," he smiled. "Maybe give it a couple of years but then I'd love to do it again. It's been so much fun."

It wasn't like I was already working out our budget for two years' time based on the funds the follow-up show might generate, but I was excited. Sadly, once again there was a manager who seemed a lot less keen than the performer was, and so nothing has yet materialised. Recently when I was walking the dog with Ben he said, "I'm sure that was Russell Howard," when a guy disappeared around a corner. It wasn't like I could chase after him and say, "Excuse me, mate, was just wondering if you'd be up for doing another gig in Taunton," especially with all the social distancing measures that are currently in place. That's a different story altogether, and one that I will come back to.

We have been extremely fortunate with some of the support we've had, and this includes some very generous help from local businesses. A rare piece of networking from me actually led to a fantastic partnership. I was put in touch with the business manager of the local Santander branch because I knew the bank did a community fund programme and I thought maybe ours would be a cause they would be interested in supporting. The way things tend to go more often than not, I was expecting him to listen attentively then tell me he'd be in touch, but it would be months before I'd hear anything if I did at all. It was the total opposite. He told me that the bank offer match funding for anything their staff raise through events for a charity they support and offered to organise a fun day in the local branches, through which the proceeds would go to us and they would match whatever was raised.

"Er . . . okay! That would be fantastic!" I smiled, not quite believing what I was hearing. It seemed the guy was inspired by our charity, as what began as an idea for a fun day in the branch became a huge outdoor fun day for the whole community; anyone who wanted to come along. Stand Against Violence were the main focus, and the whole day raised around £5,000. This was incredible, and I later learnt that the manager had been sending e-mails and calling in favours around the clock to try and ensure that the event was a success. It was just so humbling to see his enthusiasm for helping us, and how he had given up a lot of his own time to do so. I would have understood completely if putting so much energy into the event had meant he had fallen behind with his own work and he had to catch up, but instead of quitting while he was ahead he actually offered to put on three more events throughout the year, each organised by a different member of staff.

We were incredibly lucky to find him, and Santander's support was astonishing. He even offered to help run our annual ball, and make sure different members of the local corporate sector were there, in the hope that it would lead to further fundraising opportunities. I felt emotional when I made my speech during the fun day, as I always do when people go out of their way to help us. I had no idea what would happen when the campaign began, and it has far surpassed all of my expectations. Stand Against Violence would never have got so far without the support of these individuals who go out of their way for us.

We also had great support from Claims Consortium, a local firm who a friend of Lloyd's worked for. Instigating their support for us was a lasting positive impact. The CEO, Jeremy, is someone I've developed a fantastic relationship with, and he has helped a lot both professionally with claims and personally with great advice on time management and wellbeing. Claims Consortium showed wonderful dedication from the beginning and would donate an annual amount to us each year as well as organising fundraisers. To have them on board gave us financial peace of mind, especially knowing there was an amount we could count on each year, and it really helped us to develop as a charity. Two of our current trustees are senior directors for Claims Consortium, and several of their staff have volunteered for us in the past. They are another vital supporter who we would most definitely have been worse off without.

I always wanted to make sure our volunteers were rewarded for what they did, and any we were able to take on as employees we did—if they wanted to be employed with us, of course. We wanted our volunteers to be able to gain experience, qualifications, and skills that would help them going forward, and if we invested in them in this way we believed that they would return the favour with their continued support. If it felt like they were taken for granted they would most likely move on before too long. Sometimes when a paid role has come up we have not needed to advertise, as if someone is willing to work for you for free and shows dedication as well as capability then how valuable will they be to you as a paid employee, when they can give you more of their time? Dedicated volunteers are hard to find, because most people can't afford to give up their time for free, and many don't want to, but you get these rare individuals who are so dedicated that you must fight tooth and nail to keep them if you find them. That's how an excellent fundraising coordinator and bookings coordinator came to be a part of our charity, and hopefully there will be more like them in the future.

The youth branch of the charity is something we've worked hard trying to develop, and we thought we had found a way when the local council conducted a survey of young people in the town. Their feedback was that a lot of youths wanted an indoor space to hang out in rather than parks or street corners; just a safe and warm space. If we could provide this we could engage them at the same time, and so I discussed the possibility of running a youth café with the family. To my delight, they gave their full backing to the idea straight away, and we had financial backing that would remain in place as long as young people would attend. We were giving them exactly what they said they wanted. Young people had complained that there was nothing for them to do in the town and there was no safe place they could meet up. We would be providing all of this, so surely it couldn't fail.

I put the idea of employing two team leaders to the board, because if we were going to make this work we would need dedicated individuals whose position would be secure, both for us and for them. They agreed, and so we began advertising for the role. I was hoping to employ younger people, who would be able to relate well to the people who would be using the café. Also, it was notoriously difficult for young people to be given opportunities like this, and we wanted to show the belief that we wished had been shown in us when we were younger and in the same boat. Unfortunately, our gamble didn't pay off.

We were very impressed with two particular candidates during the interviews, who had both shown great enthusiasm as well as bringing excellent ideas to the table. We were excited to offer them the job, but neither maintained the same level of drive much beyond the interview. It was such a shame because they were both clearly keen for the opportunity and could have used it as a springboard for a career, their story inspiring others to take over the role later on, but one left after just a few months and the other not long afterwards.

To be fair, one did set up a fairly popular music night, but he put every ounce of his effort into this, and the rest of the time the place was pretty much empty, even though part of the role was promotion. Few seemed to know about the café, and if it remained empty the council wouldn't continue to fund us in order to keep it open. We had thrown our new employees in at the deep end a little, but they were essentially tasked with setting up a place that they and their friends would want to hang out in and were being paid to do so. They had our support and could ask us questions, but we ended up supporting to the extent that we were basically doing their job for them. It was not at all sustainable and we were pretty angry because they had both shown such potential in their interviews but seemed to prove that they hadn't been genuine and were just telling us what we wanted to hear.

The whole experience made it feel like a risk to give an opportunity to someone so young again, which may seem judgemental, but we had been trying for a number of years to reach young people and it was important to make a success of this opportunity. This meant we had to play it safer with the next candidate. We interviewed a lady who was the ripe old age

of 28, same as me, and so we hoped she was still young enough for the
kids to relate to but would have a more mature attitude towards the role.
It turned out I went to the same school as her, and we seemed to share a
vision for what the café should be, so we basically gave it to her and said,
"It's yours," allowing her free rein to put her ideas into practice. She hit
the ground running and was wise enough to realise that the music nights
had been successful, so looked to develop this side of things. She over-
hauled everything, and young people began to engage more. It looked like
it was really going to take off.

Of course it couldn't last, and the poor girl had the most ridiculous
piece of bad luck, which I felt could only happen to someone associated
with us. With the creative aspect in mind, she was keen to rebrand the café
with a new name that reflected this side of things. She came up with the
idea to call it ISIS, after the Egyptian god of society, creativity, and peace.
It was also an acronym, meaning Inspiring Social Innovation Society. We
thought it was a great idea, and she had a logo designed along with some
promotional materials with the ISIS name displayed. We were excited and
began to distribute the material far and wide around the town. Barely a
month later there were troubling reports in the news of a terrorist movement in the Middle East that was striking fear into the hearts of the local
people. They had also beheaded British and American citizens. Everyone
was horrified. This organisation seemed to embody pure evil and was rarely
off the front pages of the news. What was their name? ISIS!

When I heard this it was almost like my open jaw had to be prised shut
again, like my fingers had to be prised from the abseiling rope. What had
we done to deserve such misfortune? There were complaints, there were
e-mails, there were letters and phone calls from concerned locals. For a
while, we spent most of our working hours trying to reassure people that
we were running a youth café and not recruiting terrorists. It became exhausting very quickly, but to change the name and produce new promotional materials would have cost money we simply didn't have, and so we
just had to aim for damage limitation. We tried using the full name with
ISIS in brackets, but the level of grief we got stayed the same and so we

just had to keep explaining ourselves. People couldn't believe we'd chosen that name in light of what was going on in the world, but we had to patiently explain time and time again that the name had been chosen before ISIS became known to the world at large.

They say there's no such thing as bad publicity but "they" should try accidentally picking the name of a terrorist organisation for their new youth café. They would soon realise that bad publicity is very much a thing! Sadly, despite a valiant effort from the manager to get things going, the café was something that not enough people engaged with. This meant funding was discontinued. Just before we closed there was an interview in the newspaper with a local young lad who complained about the lack of youth provision in Taunton, which was quite maddening. We couldn't have done a lot more to promote what we were doing; there were school visits, flyers going everywhere, online promotions, and a feature in the newspaper, but the level of engagement was very disappointing.

We had the space for two to three days a week and paid quite an extortionate fee for rent, but not even this gave us exclusive access to the venue. There would often be a double booking on the days we were there, with artists hosting exhibitions or something similar. After we closed, the venue bought our equipment and furniture back from us at a knock-down price; we got £1,000, but for items that cost a lot more. At least we got something, but towards the end, we were basically paying their rent and got so little in return. It was just another instance where we were taken advantage of.

All the bad luck we've had as a charity has made me quite cynical about opportunities and about peoples' offers to help, but when I think of the high points in our story I can't help but smile. We are getting to the point now where I could see the charity continuing without me. I have to be realistic about this possibility, because in order to take the charity further we will eventually need a full-time CEO, and I have my work at the hospital.

Besides, I told Jay that he should live his life and not be forever held back by what he did when he was eighteen. Maybe it would be hypocritical of me to tell him this if I wasn't prepared to do the same someday. Moving on doesn't mean forgetting about Lloyd or abandoning everything I've worked so hard for. It means having faith in the legacy I've worked to create and handing over the reins to people I know will be able to take it further. We were getting pretty close to that point until this year, when an event that nobody saw coming put a spanner in the works, to put it mildly.

The Global Pandemic

Just when the work of Stand Against Violence seemed to be settled, with a great team in place and a firm plan for the future, there was the small matter of a global pandemic to deal with. It was absolutely unprecedented in our lifetime, and it scuppered everyone's plans for the year, both in a personal and in a professional sense. It was quite fitting for our story so far, but it meant all of our plans were on hold for the foreseeable future. On the surface, life had become pretty good for me. My nursing career was going brilliantly. I had been employed as an Advanced Clinical Practitioner, of which there are only 300 in the country, and I worked at Musgrove Park Hospital in Taunton three days a week, devoting the rest of the time to the charity and to my home life.

Ben is now my husband; we live in Bath and we have a very cute dog. Everything was going along pretty nicely, but then Covid-19 came along and blindsided the lot of us. Naturally, I was worried about what it would mean for the charity when talk began of social distancing, lockdown, and home-working. In recent years we had taken the precaution of building up our reserves to a reasonably substantial level. This was to ensure job security for our paid members of staff, but it ended up being a shrewd move on our part because it meant there was no immediate financial panic when everything was turned upside down. The school bookings had obviously been drying up, so it was a worry how we would be able to keep reaching people with our message, but I was more concerned in the short term about how my work at the hospital would change.

I had two weeks off near the beginning of the whole situation, and when I came back the layout of the department was changing daily. It was a very uncertain time, and the impression was that Covid-19 was here to stay, so we would have to get used to a different way of working. Being a hospital worker, there was no chance of me working from home. The 1.5-hour drive from Bath meant that I stayed in my parents' barn conversion during the days I was on shift rather than commuting each day, then I would drive back to Bath at the end of it. This meant that they could come and say hello from a distance while I was there, and I could legitimately drive there for work. I was far luckier than many in this respect. Most people were unable to see their families for months. Broomfield was unbelievably quiet during lockdown, almost as quiet as the air when I did my skydive, but not quite. I'm not much of an outdoorsy type, so the lockdown didn't actually make things seem too strange for me on the surface.

Obviously, going forward the whole social distancing situation will change the way we work as a charity, and we are prepared for it to be another 18 months before we can start working in anything like the same way we had been. I had actually been starting to plan for taking more of a back seat with the charity. Up until around 2012 Stand Against Violence, in terms of how we actually worked, was just me doing everything with a few freelancers. Now we actually have several paid members of staff: an administrator, an education lead, a bookings and sales coordinator, a fundraiser, and me as the CEO. The fundraising role is one we had struggled to get right. Firstly it was just part of my role, but I had no experience and limited time, so this was not ideal for the longer term. The first official fundraiser we employed was quite similar to the original youth café managers, in that she seemed fantastic on interview and looked more than qualified for the role on paper, but once she actually began it was a different story. She was more experienced than the young people we first employed to run the youth café, and we were anticipating an upsurge in grant funding now we had someone who could dedicate their hours to that role alone, but she spent all of her time organising her e-mails and folders without actually writing many applications.

It took a long time before it became apparent that something was wrong, because there is often a three- to six-month turnaround time for grants from when they are submitted until the time a decision is made. At first I was trusting, because I saw no reason not to be. She had excellent references and had impressed us during her interview, so I thought it would only be a matter of time before the funds started rolling in. Instead, when it came to the end of the year we were around £30,000 short of where we had been the previous year. Funding can be hard to obtain, and by their nature grant applications have a low success rate, with maybe as few as 1 in 10 actually leading to funding being obtained, but something didn't add up. I had been told a number of different reasons for the lack of success, the latest being that the apprentice fundraiser we had taken on was needing constant supervision. The idea was that the apprentice would learn from the main fundraiser, but it seemed like the apprentice was actually doing most of the work.

I asked to see some funding applications to try and establish what was going wrong but was told they were on a computer that was in for repairs due to problems with the hard drive. At first I took this at face value but then I kept hearing the same thing every time I asked and was beginning to think it was an excuse. The money to fund the role had come from a partnership we had with the Southern Co-Operative. It was a choice between seeing that money sift away over time or invest it in a member of staff who could bring in more substantial funds that could help us expand our work over the longer term. When a new member of staff joins you have to give them time to settle in, and if she had managed to at least cover her own wages in the first year we would have been satisfied that the long-term investment would be worth it, but instead, we lost money. Nothing improved over the next few months and so we had no real option but to part ways.

Luckily for us, the apprentice had shown herself to be very capable, and so she took over the main fundraising role. With the lack of funding coming in that year, we could only afford to pay her as an apprentice, but she had an excellent success rate with grant applications and so we were able to take her on as a fundraising coordinator after she had passed her exams.

When the two of us were sorting out the previous fundraising coordinator's folders we were shocked to discover that they were all empty. It had all been a smokescreen and she had basically been doing very little. I also managed to view a funding application she had written and was quite embarrassed that it had been sent on behalf of Stand Against Violence. It was clearly rushed, was full of spelling mistakes, and came across as very unprofessional. I guess if we hadn't taken her on we might not have taken on the apprentice, who would become a vital member of the team, so it could have been worse. When the apprentice became a full member of staff, she continued to succeed and even secured a grant from a notoriously difficult funder, who we are hoping will give us regular financial backing if we manage the relationship well.

She was very young, and so it was by no means certain she would stay forever. Indeed she left to go travelling a while back, but then returned around the time we became aware of Covid-19 and asked if we would have her back. She had a proven track record and I knew we would need to focus on grant applications more than ever, so it was an easy decision to welcome her back. I really hope we can keep her, or if not I hope we can find someone dedicated to take her place.

Part of our fundraising aim is to save enough to cover a new CEO's wages for 2 years, which is the amount of time we felt it would be reasonable to give someone to prove themselves in the role. It would have to be someone we really believe can move the charity forward, and ideally someone who is good at networking. I struggle to hear what someone is saying when there's a lot of background noise, so networking isn't really something that comes naturally to me. I have to say it will be strange for me to hand over the reins to somebody else, and I know I will always be involved in some way. The charity has been such a huge part of my life that I will have to ensure there is plenty to replace it with. A couple of times recently I've fallen into what would be described as bouts of depression at times when there isn't much going on, and I do wonder if taking a step back from Stand Against Violence might lead to another one, but I think as long as I'm very clear about where my life is going from there it will be a good move.

When I met Jay for the second time I guess it was akin to some kind of closure, although maybe true closure isn't something you ever experience when you lose a close family member so suddenly. I had kept in touch with Jay since our first meeting and I knew he was living in the east of the UK, so I thought it would be best for us to meet there rather than him coming over to Somerset. I had put an idea to him of us making a film together in which we would both be interviewed separately about Lloyd's death and the impact it has had on our lives, but then towards the end of the video the viewer would see that we were sitting opposite each other, then we would talk to each other. I thought this would be the most powerful way yet of explaining the impact this mindless act of violence had had, and for the viewers to see Jay and me discussing it calmly with each other shows that it is possible for people to change. They would see that he was just someone who made a terrible mistake, not a cold-blooded killer. The lesson that random outbursts of violence can have tragic consequences would be plain for all to see.

He seemed to agree with everything I suggested, and when we agreed to meet in Norwich to make the film I was feeling quite excited at the potential impact this new bit of work could have on young audiences. I didn't feel angry towards Jay for seeming to move on with his life. Neither did I feel nervous about the meeting. When the day came round I felt some familiar pangs of anxiety, and some of the feelings I'd had before I met him in prison resurfaced. Several of my colleagues would be at the meeting as well, but for some reason I decided to travel up separately from them by train. I've no idea why I did this, and it ended up adding extra stresses to the day that I could have done without. There were delays, which meant I arrived later than I had planned to and had less time to prepare myself for the meeting. Perhaps this was a good thing in a way because when I finally did arrive I started to feel a little nauseous and short of breath. I guess there was just a flicker of "What am I doing?" This guy had seemed so remorseful when I met him previously, but he was still responsible for my brother's death. Had I made a terrible mistake?

As the minutes went by and we waited for Jay to arrive my nerves intensified. Would I even recognise him? Had my mind been playing tricks on me that day in the prison? Oh wait, there he is! The moment I actually saw him my anxiety lifted and I said hello as if I was greeting an old acquaintance. I introduced him to the others and he was perfectly friendly and polite. Nothing seemed strange about it anymore, and we went inside to set up.

It was my turn to talk first, and I have to say it was the most difficult interview I've ever given. I was asked about the impact Lloyd's death had on my family while one of the guys responsible was sat right opposite me. I didn't feel intimidated in any way, in fact I was more conscious of not wanting to upset him, but I also wanted to be as honest as possible because I knew he would be too, and it would take a lot of courage for him. I was very used to talking about Lloyd, to the point that I could do so in quite a matter-of-fact way. Obviously, it remains the most upsetting thing I have ever experienced, but I have told the story so many times and to so many people that it no longer makes me well up. Talking about it in front of Jay was different, as I knew that hearing about the pain he had caused from one of the worst affected people would most likely bring a lot to the surface. After our first meeting, I believed he would remain composed throughout, but I knew he would be hurting. You may wonder why I would care what he was feeling, but what kind of a person would I be if I still harboured such hatred towards him after he'd been so brave and so compassionate to meet me face-to-face and tell me everything I wanted to know? Besides, I've only met him twice but I've found that when spending time in his company it's easy to forget the person he was. He's a nice guy. That may seem strange, but it's true.

Most people reading this book will be lucky enough not to have made a mistake when they were eighteen that defines the rest of their life and makes them a hate figure to a number of people no matter what they do from then on. I know some still have a lot of hatred towards Jay and don't believe he deserves an ounce of sympathy, but to live with such regret and the knowledge that you are hated must be extremely difficult. I don't know if any of the other guys responsible feel any remorse, but if they don't then that must be a lot easier for them.

Maybe Jay could have spent the rest of his life pretending that he had nothing to be sorry for but as he said, he knew the difference between right and wrong. He has admitted the pain he has caused, and how he wrestles with guilt at trying to live a normal life nowadays. If I'd made such a terrible mistake I honestly don't think I'd have had the courage to face the family who I had caused so much suffering towards. Even though it was me and my family who suffered because of Jay's actions I admire him for the way he has admitted his culpability, made such an effort to change his life and to tell me face-to-face how sorry he is on more than one occasion.

I did start to feel more emotional as the interview went on, especially when listening to Jay recounting his actions on the night Lloyd died. I was taken right back to the trial, and I found it quite difficult to focus on what was being said in the present. When this was over I heard for the first time in depth about what Jay's life was like growing up. This was possibly the most eye-opening experience I've had in all the time the charity has been in operation. I learnt that in the early years he had a happy childhood that was quite similar to mine in some ways, but then his mum married an abusive partner and everything changed. It got me thinking, I was lucky to grow up in a family that stayed together and were always supportive of each other. How differently might my life have turned out if my dad had left my mum and she'd then married a man who she grew to be terrified of? What if she had to leave everything and everyone she knew to escape him?

What struck me most was that the abuse only began after the wedding. Jay had considered this man to be a positive influence on his family and enjoyed some happy times with him, but within a short space of time the man became someone that made him quake with fear. When they moved away to the west country to escape him Jay felt so resentful towards this man for ruining his childhood and for bullying his mum. It left an anger burning within him that got closer and closer to the surface over the years, and before he was able to process it my brother was in the wrong place at the wrong time and lost his life. Jay's family may have escaped the man they feared, but his impact on their lives was devastating and is indirectly to blame for what happened to my family. Of course this isn't the sole reason, because Jay is unlikely to be the one who actually killed Lloyd, but he was the one who started the fight that led to Lloyd's death.

I heard that Jay's mum had sometimes woken him up in the middle of the night to sit with her just to avoid a beating, knowing that her husband wouldn't attack her in front of her child. I never experienced anything like this and can only imagine what it must have felt like. Jay was just a small boy when this was going on, and so there would have been nothing he could have done to protect his mum. I don't have any kids, but to me it feels like it should be the other way round. Parents are the ones who feel they must protect their kids, but how would his mum have known what this man was capable of? She may have feared for her life, and probably did. The knowledge of this would have made Jay feel hateful towards the man as he got older, and he did explain how he wanted to seek revenge. This wasn't something he was thinking of now, but he did say that if he saw him again all of those feelings would most likely return.

As I listened further I felt frustrated that so many kids go through the same as Jay did. Instead of having a stable and happy home, they are moved from refuge to refuge, only interacting with other kids who have been through similar life experiences. I don't know how someone is expected to grow up without a deep sense of injustice, mistrust, and anger after something like that, and this is the most tragic thing of all. How many more incidents like the one Jay was involved in will result from broken homes, abusive situations, and a side of life that children simply shouldn't have to live with. I'm not saying that people can use a bad childhood as an excuse to behave however they want to, but families who experience difficulties like this need to be shown a lot of support from the beginning, and this was exactly why I wanted to make the video. I wanted as many young people as possible who were at risk of making the same mistake Jay did to hear from him exactly why they should do all they can to try and avoid violent confrontations. I reiterate my point about the importance of young people learning about character, respect for others, and morality from an early age.

Towards the end of the interviews, Jay told me again how he wasn't sure if he deserved to have a good life now.

"I believe you are genuine in your rehabilitation," I told him. "And I do believe that everyone deserves a second chance. I want you to do all you can to have a good life."

"That's very kind of you to say, Adam," he replied. "When I first met you and you told me similar at the end of our time together I couldn't stop thinking about it. I was just amazed that you thought I deserved a second chance after what I caused, and I just thought what an incredible person you must be to even consider that."

I reached over to shake his hand, and that was the end of the interview. We continued to chat afterwards for a little bit, not about Lloyd but about normal things, and Jay helped us to pack up. Our cameraman went to get his van and Jay went with him, helping him to load everything in. I was chatting with my colleagues in the same way I would in front of anyone else, and we were even joking. It seemed so at odds with the rest of our time together, but afterwards one of my colleagues spoke to me away from everyone else.

"I get it now," she said. "Now I've actually spent time around him I can see exactly why you feel conflicted. I don't think he's putting on an act. He does seem truly sorry, and I do think he's changed."

"It can't be an act," I agreed. "It was brave of him just to agree to do this, and I'm really glad he did."

It was soon time to get my taxi to the train station for the long journey home, but before I did I went over to Jay once more.

"Have a good life," I told him and gave him a hug. He seemed to stop in his tracks, barely believing what had just happened. I'm not really sure why I did it, except that it just seemed like the best way to say goodbye. I may never know what he was thinking, but as I was getting in the taxi he appeared next to me.

"Have a safe journey home," he said as he squeezed my arm gently.

"Thanks, Jay. You, too. I'll be in touch when we've edited the videos. Thank you again for doing this."

That was that, and the process of putting the finished video together was as lengthy as these things tend to be, but we got there, and it has now been shown to many young people, including young offenders. The impact has always been positive, and I consider it to be one of our most valuable resources. I've not met Jay again since, but I was very grateful that he agreed to be involved with this book, and I hope that reading his story will have a profound impact for people.

Violence continues to be an issue in our society, and in recent times it has been brought to the forefront after an African-American man named George Floyd died when under arrest on the street and there were anti-racist demonstrations all over the world, some of which turned violent. In America especially there were riots with looting, and although I can understand the frustrations of the people who took part I disagree with their actions because ultimately violence solves nothing.

If you look through history at attempts to make genuine, lasting change happen through violence you will see that by and large it simply doesn't work. Nelson Mandela is hailed as a hero and what he was hoping to achieve was commendable, but his methods early on were violent, and many were killed as a result. Modern South Africa is still rife with tension and is quite a lawless society in places, with extreme violence being so commonplace that people living in cities have high barbed wire fences around their homes, and some even have built-in flame-throwers on their vehicles to deter carjackers! That is not even scratching the surface of the whole picture, but the point is that South Africa cannot be described as a peaceful country. I think anyone who was honest would agree. There have been many violent revolutions throughout history, and all of them have led to many more years of tensions, death, and no resolution. As far as I can see, Martin Luther King's non-violent protests arguably brought more meaningful change than any of the others I've mentioned.

Ultimately, violence will only lead to more violence. If a violent protest is shown on TV, some might sympathise with the cause but many will just see it as a senseless act, and there will always be those seeking revenge. For there to be lasting peace there simply cannot be violence. It may bring some kind of short-term and shallow changes, but it doesn't bring lasting resolution to conflict. The suffragettes, it could be argued, used violent methods but they were always aimed at simply causing disruption and not at causing harm to others.

In the UK we didn't have many violent protests, there was just a bit of a flare-up in London, but a much talked about event was the forcible removable by protesters in Bristol of the Edward Colston statue, which was then dumped in the river. I do fully support statues of individuals who perpetrated slavery and other forms of abuse being removed to museums, but I don't support them being removed altogether and disposed of. One of my favourite sayings is "Those who forget the past are doomed to repeat it," and this is relevant in so many ways. It's quite likely that many of those who showed vociferous support for the removal of the statue actually had very little idea about who Colston was, or what he did. If all trace of him is removed then it defeats the point. If the current and subsequent generations are educated about what he did and why it was wrong then these things are less likely to happen in the future.

If I had been born 20 years earlier I probably would have been attacked in the street and maybe even chemically castrated for being gay, but I have to admit that in this day and age I receive little in the way of persecution, and if this is the case then I see little sense in dwelling on past injustices. Being aware of them is of course important but remembering them and moving on is the way to go. Besides, if I was to blame heterosexual people in general nowadays for what happened in the past, even if they had done nothing wrong, then where would be the sense? Of course it is terrible what happened to peoples' ancestors, but if I can tell one of my brother's killers that he deserves a second chance while he is still quite a young man then it would be very hypocritical of me to say that the modern generation should still be blamed for the mistakes previous generations made.

That is the overall message I would wish to convey from my story and everything you have read. Violence and hatred solve nothing; only peace, a deep understanding, and empathy bring about resolution. By making peace with Jay I have allowed myself to try and move forward with my own life. Nothing he or I could ever do will bring Lloyd back, and I have worked for over a decade establishing an organisation that is dedicated to spreading the message of the impact violence can have. They will continue to do so. In which ways this happens going forward I guess will be up to the new CEO when they are in position, although if they want to shake things up too much they'll have to get past the trustees first! I am confident that the original aims of the charity will continue, no matter how much or little I have to do with the running of things directly.

It will be very strange to step down as CEO, and such a short time, relatively speaking, after I fought tooth and nail to stay in the role when there was turmoil within the board. It just goes to show that situations change, people change, and ultimately life has to move on at some point, no matter what happens. I will never forget the brother who lost his life nearly as long ago now as the number of years he was alive for. I will never forget the time I trapped his head in the clothes horse, or when he egged the other kids on to tease me at school. I will never forget the time I cleaned all of his own puke off him when he woke up in the night, or when I came to with him holding me up, thinking I was dying of a brain haemorrhage. I will never forget the time he got me to clean the bins on the way to our parents' place for Sunday lunch, or the time he reassured me he would always be my brother when I thought he might want to disown me. We had our conflicts and our disagreements but we had so much love for each other deep down, and as we were getting older we even started to show it. I will never know what other escapades, laughs, and tears we might have shared had he lived, but I do know for sure that in dying he pushed me on to become the best person I could be and to achieve more than I think I ever would have otherwise. I hope I've made you proud, Lloyd. I couldn't have been prouder to have been your brother for the short time I was allowed to be.

Reflection

The warmth of the sun is the first thing I remember. It's one of those cloudless summer days which are rare enough in England that you notice them when they arrive. I'm walking on a narrow path by the side of a beautiful country church. Everything's bathed in golden sunshine, the sky is filled with birdsong, and flowers of all colours are blooming in the hedgerows. I feel at peace, like I did during the skydive, but why am I here? I'm on my own in the middle of nowhere. As I walk alongside the church some kind of recollection surfaces. It's a special day. I round the corner and there he is, stood next to my mum. They're both absolutely beaming. Lloyd says nothing but walks straight up to me. He looks barely a day older than when I last saw him, yet he looks so grown up, and not just because of the suit he's wearing. I'd been walking towards him at the same time without even realising, and within moments he's right in front of me. He hugs me, and I hug him back, but still we say nothing. The material of his suit is baking in the sun and feels warm to the touch.

A minute later I'm still hugging him, and we remain in silence. Eventually, the realisation hits me.

"You can't be here, Lloyd," I think. "You died."

With that, I wake up in my bed. The church is gone, I'm in my room. Lloyd isn't here, but I can still feel the material of his suit and the warmth of the sun. I still can for some time. It's the strangest feeling. The first time I told anyone this was when a girl at a school where I was giving a talk asked me if I ever dream about Lloyd. I had only the once, and I could only give the briefest answer because to tell the story made me want to cry. I feel sad even writing about it now. I guess I dreamt about Lloyd's wedding day, and everything about it makes me well up. The joy he never got to experience, how happy my mum looked, how beautiful the day was. Every time I think of that dream it brings everything back, except it doesn't bring Lloyd back. Nothing will. It still seems so unfair. Now he's been dead for nearly as long as he lived for, and the pain is less intense but the grief is still there. There's always something to remind me, and I guess there always will be. That dream was so comforting, because it really felt like I was seeing Lloyd again, yet it was so upsetting because I couldn't stay there.

I told my auntie what I had dreamt at Uni the day afterwards, and we both had a cry. She made me smile with three simple words: "Life's a bitch!" It just seemed to sum up what we were feeling in the moment. When there are no words for a situation, sometimes a simple phrase like this can take the edge off things. Another time, not long after Lloyd had died, an Uncle came to the house and we stepped outside. Neither of us were really speaking, then he exhaled deeply, shook his head, and just said, "F***in' hell!"

What else could we say, really? This was no time for small talk. We both knew that something truly horrific had happened to my brother, his nephew, and there was nothing we could say to make it better. Just the shared understanding that we didn't really know what to say was encapsulated in this short phrase.

It did make us both a little more relaxed, even though nothing was relaxing at the time. Friends and family didn't really know what to say to us, but the best thing to say was just anything normal. People would leave meals on the doorstep that we could heat up, which was massively appreciated. Deciding what to cook for dinner can be hard enough at the best of times, but when you're going through such intense grief, it's wonderful to be able to just bung something in the oven that you didn't even prepare. There are ready meals, but home-cooked meals from friends were a healthier option. It was just lovely of them when I look back on it.

So I guess it's time to reflect. Sadly, I would say that the level of violence in the UK is about the same as it was 15 years ago when we started the campaign, but I guess that's not the point. If our message is going to have an impact on a generational scale it will take time, and who knows how many instances of fatal violence have been avoided through people attending our workshops? I do think the levels of violence lessened for a while, but then they increased again. Of course it is a very complex issue; people are violent for all sorts of reasons, and attacks are often not premeditated but are momentary explosions of rage that have tragic consequences. I do believe the society we live in is partly to blame. I would say that on the whole, people have less respect for each other than they used to.

Gang culture is also very different nowadays to how it once was. Feared gangsters of yesteryear such as The Krays, as far as I understand, used to fight rival gangs and tended to leave civilians alone as long as they didn't cause them any trouble. Nowadays you have gangs of lawless young people who seem to think they have nothing to lose and will "shank" a passer-by as a mark of respect among their fellow members. This is a major problem in some areas of the larger cities mostly but is not exclusively an urban issue. The older generation still had a sense of moral fibre and respect for others, because that was the way they were brought up, but nowadays I see an increasing lack of boundaries or ideas of right and wrong that are instilled from a young age. Schools have very limited power nowadays to discipline bullies, and with a continued lack of life skills education, I can only see this leading to more kids growing up with no respect or morals. The majority will still grow up to be decent people, but those who need the most guidance are not always getting it, which can lead to incidents that ruin lives.

When I stop to think about my whole story, I can't help but feel that all I have achieved is somewhat bittersweet. If I was simply to state a fact, then nearly all I have achieved both personally and professionally since 2005 happened because Lloyd died. Also the deeper I think about it all the more troubling it seems, because it's conceivable that many lives could have been saved because of his death. Attending our workshop and being able to see violence in a different light, or just hearing about Lloyd's story another way, could have changed the way a lot of young people think and could have stopped a lot of other incidents from taking place that would otherwise have led to fatalities. Jay became the better person he admits he is today because of the fallout of what he caused through starting that fight. The fact of the matter is that a lot of positive things have come about as a result of my brother dying. It is a fact I can't deny, and it is very difficult to contemplate. There is a conflict in my mind about the whole thing. It would be false of me to say otherwise, even though it isn't very socially acceptable of me to do so. Would I have achieved as much if he had lived? I honestly don't know.

When I was attacked a few months before Lloyd was it didn't inspire me to start a campaign, even though I was the one who was beaten black and blue. I literally had the scars to prove that violence was an issue, but I just wanted to try and forget about it. It took a loss of life to inspire me to action. For over a decade I didn't look back and put all of my energy into setting up Stand Against Violence, taking the message as far and wide as I could in the hope that it would prevent suffering. I would never have done that if Lloyd hadn't died. An event like that is always going to have a profound impact on the lives of the family, and I'm glad I took the path I did rather than allowing it to make me a lifelong recluse.

To draw this to a close I guess all I can do is bring everything full circle. One night in September 2005, I received a phone call from my dad. The call woke me up, and I was pretty annoyed about it. Of course if I'd known what he was about to tell me I would have been a lot kinder. He told me that my younger brother, Lloyd, had been killed by a group of youths in a random attack. This was quite difficult to process, as you may imagine. I knew straight away that my life would be different from now on, and I started a campaign to try and make people aware of this and other violent incidents that were tearing families apart, and the need to put a stop to them.

Over the years this campaign became a charity, and I believe we have succeeded many times over in our aim of educating people about the impact of violence, in the hope of preventing at least one family from going through the same thing we did. There is no real way of quantifying this, seeing as if we were successful in our aims we would never hear about the violent incidents that were avoided by young people being inspired to change their ways because these incidents would not happen. Judging by feedback we've received I truly believe that we have inspired many to think about the consequences of their actions, and so may well have prevented a number of tragic incidents. I am proud of where the charity is now, but we have certainly faced a lot of setbacks along the way. Some have been minor, such as not quite seeing eye to eye with the local police on every issue, some have been major, such as accidentally naming our youth café after a terrorist organisation.

A popular daytime TV star has become our patron, Her Majesty the Queen told me face-to-face that our work was important, I learnt through a fundraising endeavour that the only time I feel truly is at peace is when I jump out of a plane. We were featured on the Taunton Monopoly board, our videos have been seen by more young people than you could fit in the gardens of Buckingham Palace, one of our trustees was disrespected by a young rap star but she took it in her stride and put him in his place. Our board went through changes and came out the other side thriving. We raised a lot of funds, we missed out on a lot of funds, people gave a lot of their time to us and expected nothing in return, but others in a position of influence wouldn't help us when it would have been little bother for them to do so.

Oh, and last but definitely not least, I met one of the men who was responsible for Lloyd's death. I half expected him to say something obviously false about how sorry he was before trying to get me to put in a good word for his parole hearing. Instead, I met a pleasant young man who had done a lot of soul-searching over the years and was genuinely remorseful for his actions.

It's been quite a journey. Sorry for using that cliché, but sometimes there are no better words than the obvious ones. I do feel uncomfortable even now receiving praise, but I have to admit that I'm proud of what I've achieved. It began as Lloyd's legacy, but it's also mine. I suppose I should thank him again for dying, and what he allowed me to become by doing so. Also the number of people who have been educated about the impact of violence as a result of what happened. Lloyd's death has had a number of positive impacts, and I can't deny that, but would I give all of it up if it meant I could go back and allow him to have lived?

Of course I would. He was my brother.

Reflections from Tracy Casson, Education and Training Lead for Stand Against Violence

I will say right at the outset that I was very unsure about the whole idea of the Adam and Jay meeting. Jay was a murderer—he had killed Lloyd, hurt the Fouracre family beyond all imagination and now we were giving him the opportunity to hurt Adam all over again. To me, there were a whole heap of reasons as to why this was not a good idea . . .

Two years prior to the meeting set up by Adam I had joined the charity he established but had first met the Fouracres when I was offered a maternity cover teaching post at a small school in a village just outside of Taunton. Lloyd was one of my pupils. A very easy-going young lad who always had a great big smile on his face. One particularly fond memory I have of Lloyd is the occasion I glanced up from a book to check the class was okay only to see him "twirling" round and round in my classroom before looking at me and giving me a great big grin. Why he was twirling I do not know and as far as I was concerned, because of Jay I now never would.

I can still remember the day I saw the announcement of Lloyd's murder on the TV. As I often tell the pupils I talk to on behalf of the charity, it is a bit like the response people have when someone famous dies—people can tell you exactly where they were and what they were doing at the time they found out. Well, I can do the same with Lloyd. I was sitting on the floor of my lounge playing with an empty lemonade bottle, the chew toy of choice of my pet Rottweiler. I can remember being pounced on by this large and happy dog. He had seen that the bottle stopped moving in mid-air, as I realised that this horrible story which was causing me to feel a huge blow somewhere deep inside my stomach was about Lloyd, the twirling young boy with the big grin. The happy lad who did not deserve this.

The day came, and we left Taunton for the long journey to meet Jay. It was summertime and I can remember sitting in a very stuffy van feeling quite "hot and bothered" inside about the whole thing. I was determined not to like Jay, although Adam had said before I might well be surprised, but no. After leaving the primary school I had eventually gone on to work with "hard to reach" young people, as Jay would have been referred to by those in certain areas of authority, so I thought I knew what to expect . . . nothing about Jay could shock me . . . little did I know!

After a long journey, not helped by holiday traffic, we arrived at our destination. Adam was due to join us later that evening, having travelled separately from a different destination, but we had exchanged a few texts and I knew that everything was going to plan. He would be there ready for the interview the next day. We had prepared some questions in advance and knew what each of us were doing so there was nothing left to do but wait and imagine what the next day would bring.

There were five of us involved in this day: Adam, myself, Carly our education trustee, and Mike the cameraman, plus of course Jay. We had hired a quiet venue in which to do the filming, so set off early to get things set up . . . and then waited for our guest to arrive. We all seemed a bit quiet at this point. It was a strange atmosphere, one of anticipation with an un-sureness about how this would go mixed with an unspoken protectiveness between Carly and myself towards Adam. It seemed like forever and then Adam looked at his phone. The text had arrived to say Jay was downstairs and Adam went to collect him . . . the moment had arrived.

I remember seeing Adam return up the galleried staircase with Jay following behind. Adam introduced everyone and we sat down to begin. I don't really know what I was expecting at this stage, but I remember believing beforehand that I would somehow know right from the start that he was different . . . he was a murderer and there was no way I would be fooled into thinking he was okay now just because he said he had changed . . . I was determined not to be fooled but to find the truth behind this. However, as I sat down and looked directly at Jay, I was hit with the realisation that he didn't look like a murderer . . . quite what a murderer looks like, what identifying features I expected them to have, I wasn't sure. I was sure Jay would have something about him and I would instantly know . . . but he just didn't. I had to grudgingly admit to myself that if I stood next to him in the supermarket I would not "know." There was nothing that set him apart from any other member of the public.

Undeterred by this I decided to focus all my attention on trying to catch him out in what he said, so I sat listening very carefully to his words and at the same time looked for giveaway signs to show that he was not genuine. In my school days, a teacher had once said that "the eyes are the windows to the soul" and so I looked hard for my answer. I looked at his body language, tracked eye movements when he spoke to see if it was something he was recalling from a script, fidgeting, rubbing his nose, etc. In fact, I tried everything I had ever read, either fact or fiction, about ways to tell if someone is lying.

The conclusion I came to? He wasn't.

I felt sure that Jay was genuine in his remorse and had realised the enormity of what he had done. In actual fact it seemed on some level he was appalled with himself at even the idea that he was ever capable even of doing it, let alone that he did. I do believe that it is a memory that will haunt him for the rest of his life; a split-second choice he made as a young lad in the heat of the moment, like so many other split-second choices, but this one with devastating consequences that will live with him forever.

However, I believe for Jay there will be an even greater depth to that now by Adam's response at the end of the interview. Adam thanked Jay and empathised about how hard the day must have been for him (even though Adam had to relive his own nightmare through Jay's eyes). He told Jay that *he* believed he was genuine in his rehabilitation and deserved a second chance at life . . . and then offered him his hand to shake! Jay looked so shocked at this gesture; a gesture with far more impact than can be put into words. Something offered by someone who has had so much taken from them and been caused so much pain towards the man who was responsible. It was remarkable—heartbreaking and yet inspiring all at the same time.

I left that day feeling privileged to have witnessed it. To see two young men whose lives had been brought together in such an unimaginable way, both working together to help others to avoid the pain and suffering that they have experienced in different ways because of that fateful day all those years ago.

As for me? Well, I now understand what Adam meant. I was surprised. I could find no reason to think Jay was not genuine. I explored and yet exhausted all of my doubts until I had to admit defeat. I realised that the Jay I was looking at knew he had made a snap decision as a young lad, like so many others, but his snap decision had far-reaching consequences. He didn't try to say otherwise but showed a true acceptance of his deeds and total remorse. How many people reading this will remember things they did in their teens they regret and wished they hadn't? Jay is no different. His mistake at that point was much bigger than those of most people, but he has taken responsibility for his young self and his actions back then and is working hard to be a better person. My choice having been on this journey is now, like Adam, I believe that Jay is genuine in his regret for the past and his desire to be a better person in the future. He does deserve a second chance.

Reflections from Carly Anderson, Stand Against Violence Trustee

I began teaching 17 years ago in 2003. At 21 I was enthusiastic and keen to prove myself. I took up my first role in a school that had a reputation for being challenging. My first lesson saw the group throw all the tables and chairs around the room and a barrage of foul language was thrown in my direction. I stuck it out, and although hard work, the reward of knowing that once you gained the trust of these pupils you could make a difference is immeasurable to any of position I have taken since.

It was during my time here that I contacted Adam Fouracre. I was aware of the devastating events leading to Lloyd's death and was inspired by the article I had read about his work and the Anne Frank award he had received.

At this time I was a year 10 tutor and many of the young people I was working with had become involved with fights inside and outside of school. They had often expressed knowledge that this was not the way to solve issues but felt they had no choice or that this was just the way things were done. They did not think past the immediate event, nor consider any consequences.

I had been tasked with arranging a crash day event, an off-timetable day where the students took part in sessions around a theme, and I had decided that this was a pattern of behaviour worth addressing. I e-mailed Adam, not really expecting a response or indeed knowing if he would think it an appropriate request given how these issues had affected him.

I was bowled over to receive a response and together we planned for the day. He started by speaking to the whole year group, using what now seems like a fairly primitive PowerPoint, given the nature of SAV's resources today, but nonetheless the whole year group hung on every word he said, and as the home video of Lloyd played and the photo of Lloyd disappeared from the photos with his friends, I could see the reality of the situation becoming relatable to the pupils around me. Adam then spent time with each tutor answering the difficult and often emotive questions of the pupils. As I have had the pleasure of keeping in touch with many of these pupils from my first and very special tutor group, I know that over a decade later this is something they still remember.

On the day Adam and I both recognised the potential for change that sessions like these could have for young people and this is where my relationship with SAV began. We hired out the local YMCA and planned a similar event for other local school children to attend. The response from all involved was positive and we quickly snowballed this into a whole day of anti-violence education, including self-defence, first aid, and further conflict resolution. The whole time Lloyd's story was at the heart of everything.

Over time, the PowerPoint became a film, and the sessions became carefully constructed interactive activities. We began to take these sessions into schools and even started to train up other teachers to deliver them.

At times I found myself questioning my involvement. Working from a temporary office in the top floor of a church and transporting a giant screen and box of iPads halfway across the country to deliver an hour-long session was challenging and difficult to do whilst I was also raising three tiny children. However, during every session I witnessed the positive attitude change of the young people we worked with. I could never bring myself to stay away from SAV's work for long and found myself agreeing to a number of Adam's pleas across the years. Anything from designing free downloadable resources, training peer teachers, visiting young offenders, heading off to Ashford young offenders' prison, cinema adverts, planning new workshops, teacher training, and now to my current efforts as education trustee.

It was during this role that I found myself involved in one of the most emotionally draining and yet inspiring moments of my teaching career. Adam had agreed to meet Jay, one of Lloyd's attackers, and had at that time set the wheels in motion for him to work with SAV upon his release. I think everyone doubted this would happen, but at the same time dared to think about how this could be inspirational to many of the toughest young people we come into contact with.

When the time finally arrived, Jay stuck to his promise and agreed to film an interview. Tracy, the now full-time SAV teacher, and I set off with the TV producer in his white van to meet Adam at the filming location. It was a journey I won't forget for many reasons. Maybe it was the closeness of three people, one a complete stranger, sharing the bench seat of a van, or arriving at the hotel to find Adam had us booked in for the wrong night, but it was probably because of the situation itself. How would anyone feel knowing they were going to meet with a murderer? Not to mention the pressure to do this right, to emotionally support Adam, to be dignified towards Jay. Although a murderer, he is still a man, and a man that had agreed to relive his life's biggest regret in front of us under the glare of the spotlight with a camera in his face. We also had to ensure the video would be suitable to support the important work of the charity. The pressure really was on.

We worked all day, and we battled all day with the strange feeling that Jay was a nice person. In the back of all our minds was the overwhelming confirmation we were looking for that people are capable of remorse, and that people are capable of change. In this, we also found a huge amount of guilt. This man had killed an innocent person, and yet here we were forgiving him.

For me, watching Adam wrestle with this more than any of us was something I will never forget. Seeing him shake hands with this person was so inspiring because he could recognise that if we want to really stand for all that we say we do, we have to put that into action and show young people that it is not too late to change.

Listening to Jay also made me reflect on things. He didn't make excuses for what he did, he owned his actions but at the same time I could understand how he had got to that point. It saddened me to listen to some of the events of his past, and it left me with a greater empathy, that I will carry with me in the future for those who have struggled with life's challenges.

After the interview, we had to fight our way out of town with all the equipment on foot as the town centre had closed for the mayor's parade. Jay volunteered to help and led us to the taxi park. We left him with a smile. He was about to start a new life, with a baby on the way and we were excited at the prospects of how today's effort might positively inspire others. That was a good feeling but still a moment of great sadness knowing that with a different turn of fate and a few small actions changed this was a moment that may never have happened.

In order to do my part in changing the path for someone else, so that another young person like Lloyd, or as some might say, Jay, might not become a victim I will continue to support the work of SAV and take great pride in all we have achieved so far.

Thank-Yous

To Ben, you have kept me grounded, been the voice of reason and balance, and kept me feeling loved and safe.

My family, who have always been there in the background offering words of encouragement and support.

To those who have come and gone bringing into my life new inspiration, passion, and faith that I could achieve my objectives. There are too many to mention. Your influence has been significant and always timely, without you I could have lost hope, drive, or never discovered the strength I could have.

To those who contributed to the obstacles and challenges, looking back I am grateful. Challenges and setbacks have only made me and the charity stronger and more determined to succeed. Your contributions have been invaluable.

Finally, I must thank Jay Wall, who has shown great strength and courage to share his story with us. He is not "The Bad Guy" but someone who has made a catastrophic mistake and has paid the price. He has learnt from his mistakes, and together we hope this story—Lloyd's story, our story—can open people's eyes to the risks and consequences of mindless violence.

A Final Word

All I can say is that I am mum to two incredible young men. Adam never ceases to amaze me. Seeing him grow from a shy, insecure young man to this confident speaker has been incredible.

– Helen Fouracre, Adam and Lloyd's mum

About the Authors

Adam Fouracre founded Stand Against Violence when he was 18 years old, following his brother's murder in 2005. Alongside his work with the charity, he is a qualified nurse with an MSc in Advanced Practice and works as an Advanced Clinical Practitioner in Emergency Medicine at Musgrove Emergency Department, Taunton. Adam lives in Bath, Somerset, with his husband, Ben, and their little pooch, Tilly.

Dave Urwin is a part-time author and ghostwriter from Somerset, England. He became the Community Funding and Development Officer for Stand Against Violence in 2020 after helping Adam to write this book.